Big Boom's Autograph Page

I'm trying to understand this thing called Heaven. At this point I think we spend our whole lives trying to find the key to open the Pearly Gates. I think we are looking for the wrong thing. Maybe it is not the key that opens the door. God may ask you a question instead. I think the question should be, "What have you done for me lately?"

To:

From:

Also by Big Boom

If You Want Closure in Your Relationship,
Start with Your Legs

How to Duck a Suckah

A Guide to Living a Drama-Free Life

BIG BOOM
THE BODYGUARD FOR WOMEN'S HEARTS

A Fireside Book
Published by Simon & Schuster
New York   London   Toronto   Sydney

FIRESIDE
A Division of Simon & Schuster, Inc.
1230 Avenue of the Americas
New York, N Y 10020 .

Copyright © 2008 by Big Boom Freeman

First Fireside trade paperback edition January 2008

FIRESIDE and colophon are registered trademarks of Simon & Schuster, Inc.

Designed by Jamie Kerner Scott

Manufactured in the United States of America

1   3   5   7   9   10   8   6   4   2

Library of Congress Cataloging-in-Publication Data
Boom, Big.
   How to duck a suckah : a guide to living a drama-free life / Big Boom.
      p.   cm
1. Man-woman relationships. 2. Interpersonal relations. 3. Men—
Psychology. I. Title.
HQ801.B7527 2008
646.7'7082—dc22

2007027934

ISBN-13: 978-1-4165-4653-5
ISBN-10: 1-4165-4653-7

This book is dedicated to my lovely wife, Lauren,
who's the spirit of my life. Thank you for your constant
support of my work, for listening patiently even when
I'm sure you didn't want to, and for always believing in me.
I am committed to you. I love you.

To Hasani, my precious treasure.
You amaze me every day.
Being your dad is the greatest reward.

I would like to dedicate this book to those ladies who
realized I was a suckah in my days, when I didn't realize
I was one. My prayer is to hope that each lady has found
forgiveness and love, and has made the difficult choice to
become better and not bitter. It's my prayer that you see
I'm a changed man and hear my meaningful message.

Dear Reader,

Boom and I share a great friendship and marriage. The struggle between two strong minds sometimes brought friction in our relationship, but little did we dream where we'd be today.

I look at him now and remember where he came from. Boom has changed drastically, learned to control the power of his thoughts and words, and freed himself from his past.

His mission is to help women find strength through adversity. He has become a God-fearing man who has fully dedicated his life to God's vision. Boom is the Bodyguard of my heart. His voice, his touch, even a quick glance in my direction, always sends shivers throughout my soul. I could not be more proud to have him as my husband.

Boom's enthusiasm for life, his family, and me is truly inspiring. I am blessed to have him in my life. I can trust and depend on his protection and his honesty—even when I may not want to hear it. He's strengthened my own faith and ability to hope, believe and dream.

We have put God first and this has made our friendship and marriage stronger and our home happier. We have come to know the true treasure of a great relationship. I hope that by reading this book you, too, will be on your way to knowing your worth and the relationship you deserve.

Sincerely,
Lauren Freeman

Acknowledgments

Most important, I thank God for using me as a vessel to continue to deliver words of inspiration, truth, and personal transformation.

Big thanks to Touchstone Fireside publisher Mark Gompertz, who made *If You Want Closure in Your Relationship, Start with Your Legs* come to life by sending Cherise Davis out to hear me speak and for believing so passionately and showing your enthusiasm and excitement for this project. I want to personally thank you. Big love.

Big thanks to Sulay Hernandez, my editor, for all her dedication, passion, and true love for my vision. Thank you for understanding the way I think and helping me to put my words and thoughts on paper. Big love.

Big thanks, to Shida Carr, my publicist. You are the *best*! Your time, hard work, and dedication have brought me to the forefront of the media world. Thank you again for keeping me on track. Big love.

Big thanks to Shawna Lietzke, to the sales and marketing team at Simon & Schuster, and to art director Cherlynne Li, for working so hard to support my vision and dream.

Big thanks to Rushion McDonald, my manager and true friend, a man who works on my career even when he should be sleeping, a man of many words who keeps his, a man who always calls to give, never to borrow. Thank you for believing in my vision and dream. Let's go make that money! Big love.

Big thanks to Steve Harvey, my friend, a man who knows how to get you from the back to the front. I am grateful and blessed for the many long years of our friendship and working relationship. He is a friend who has taught me that life is full of bumps and bruises and that you can still make a stand even if you fall down. Big love.

Big thanks to Larry Barnes, my best friend since grade school. No matter how many times I think that I was right, he knows the right time to tell me that I was wrong. Thank you for all your support over the many years and for still believing in my dream. Big love.

Big thanks to Bishop T.D. Jakes, my spiritual adviser, who has proved to me that the book he teaches from is my guiding light. Big love.

Big thanks to Sylvia Johnson, my prayer warrior. Special thanks for all your hard work, long hours, dedication, time, support, and for always believing in my work being a masterpiece. Big love.

Big thanks to Joseph Adamo and Lombardo Custom Apparel, for your passion for fashion—keeping me looking so debonair and helping me stay on top of the fashion game. Big love.

Big thanks to attorney Ricky Anderson, for making sure my i's are dotted and my t's are crossed and making sure I get the best deal and helping me keep my mouth clean from talking bad about somebody that should not be in my business. Big love.

Big thanks to the Waller family, for helping me accomplish one of my dreams, and for support and always finding humor in me. Big love.

Big thanks to my family and friends for supporting and listening when you probably didn't want to and for your prayers, love, and undying enthusiasm. I recognize that not everyone is so blessed with family and friends as loving or as true. Big love.

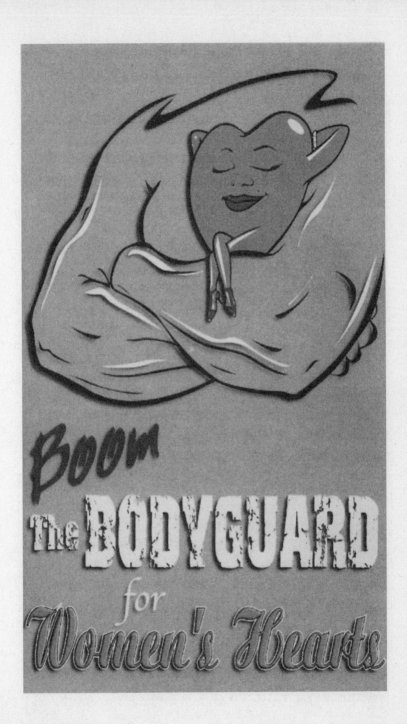

Boom

The BODYGUARD

for

Women's Hearts

ENGLISH

Bodyguard for women's hearts

ARABIC

حارس لقلوب النساء "Hares lekolob el nessaa"

SPANISH

el guardaespaldas para corazones de mujeres

FRENCH

garde du corps des cœurs des femmes

GERMAN

Leibwächter für Frauenherzen

ITALIAN

la guardia del corpo del cuore delle donne

DUTCH

De lijfwacht voor de harten van vrouwen

PORTUGESE

o guarda-costas dos corações das mulheres

RUSSIAN

Телохранитель женских сердец

NORWEGIAN

Bodyguard for kvinner hjerter

TRADITIONAL CHINESE

保鏢為婦女的心臟

KOREAN

여자 심혼을 위해 보디가드

JAPANESE

女性の中心のボディーガード

GREEK

σωματοφυλακή για τις καρδιές των γυναικών

Contents

A Note from the Author

The reason I named this book *How to Duck a Suckah* is that most women I know are sitting ducks. I want to give you the tools to use so you can become more powerful and still have fun. Let's just look at it this way: When you're a duck in the woods, just minding your own business, sooner or later the hunter will come along. Men are always looking for something to catch or shoot down. You are going to be his target one day. All you are doing is enjoying your day, just floating in the water, thinking about love, and men are thinking about capturing you. This is why I describe some women as sitting ducks.

How to Use
How to Duck a Suckah

Relax: Get yourself a glass of wine or your favorite beverage. Find a quiet place to read and give yourself a few moments to relax completely. Camouflage the title of your book, just in case your loved one walks in, so that it doesn't cause a problem in your relationship. Because *all men* know that knowledge is *power.* Take a deep breath, get comfortable, and clear your mind.

Read: Once you are ready, allow yourself enough time so you can really concentrate on each insight, without feeling rushed or hurried. Then read each insight slowly and carefully.

Think: Spend a few moments analyzing and considering what you are reading, and then repeat or paraphrase it out loud to yourself. Understand the importance of each insight.

Apply: Welcome each new insight and idea and then put these ideas into practice. Use them daily in your own life. Think of ways to strengthen and change your life as well as your relationship.

Introduction

How to Duck a Suckah is not the average self-help book, nor is it a simulation pity party for women. It is a relationship guide for women who need to know and learn how to help themselves. The title of this book and its content address what many women think but don't say. If this sounds too good to be true, please read on.

My inspiration for *How to Duck a Suckah* comes from hundreds of women. I've spent years of hearing women complain, appear drained, look stressed, and agonize over men. I've met these types of women at resorts, spas, clubs, parties, benefits, social events, work, and casual affairs. I've also met them on the streets, in malls, in restaurants, at seminars, on TV shows, and at radio stations, and a few of them are women I've been directly involved with throughout my life. Women are expressing their pains of how they got used and abused by someone they trusted, loved, and adored.

After listening to many women complaining for the better part of their lives, I'm convinced there are some pretty hard-up women out there. Not only do they make men think they are dumb, they make other women think they are desperate for anything (good or bad) a man has to offer.

Every woman has at some point in time had a man pursue her, only to lose interest in her the minute she lets him in her heart, mind, and body. Every woman knows what it feels like to be taken advantage of. They know what it feels like to be used. These problems are so common to women that relationship help is a booming business. This is true for married and single women alike.

So why do women make such bad choices in men? I wondered why women didn't just make better choices. I have met so many women since I wrote my last book, and almost every one of them has had or is having problems with men. There're too many to count. It astounds me how these seemingly smart, well-educated, professional women can't make heads or tails of how to have a successful relationship with a man. Yes, they are motivated to try and make it work like the fairy tale or the princess concept, but it is still a paradise never visited for most of them. To let the woman tell it, she knows that there is a knight in shining armor out there—she just hasn't found him yet.

I have to admit that the women who do the most complaining about men also do the most to avoid taking action to stop the bad patterns. They give up on doing better for themselves, give in to the man, or give out from stress and depression. That fact alone led me to write this book.

The day I decided to write this book was like any other day. I woke up, thanked God, looked over at my wife and asked her why she kept pushing the snooze button. She said, "How about good morning first, my friend?" I replied, "How could it be a good morning when you've pushed the snooze button at least four times?" If you just get out of bed, jump in the shower, and start your morning, you would be surprised how smooth your day will go, instead of waking your brain up and putting it back to sleep. My wife blames me for her broken sleep because I sleep with the TV on. Not because I'm afraid of the dark, it's just that my mind will not turn off.

Once that part of my morning was over, I drank a huge bottle of water, took a shower, and started my day. I had breakfast with my family—most of the time it's with my daughter because my wife is usually still upstairs changing clothes two or three times trying to get dressed for work. After breakfast, I go to my office inside my head. People say that I'm crazy. This is usually how it happens for me. I wake up from dreams and deep thoughts with an idea and I immediately start talking into my recorder. I guess you could say this book is a little bit of many books rolled into one.

Sometimes it's so hard for me to listen to a woman complain about the same problems over and over. She starts out talking about positive things and how good her life is, and then somewhere in the conversation she starts venting about her man and her relationship problems, or not having a man. And, if she does have one, she complains about him not being a good man. Each time it's the same problem with a different woman and man.

Because of the vicious cycle, I began a journey to try and figure out why. First I asked myself a few questions: Is the whole truth and nothing but the truth being told? Is it really always the man's fault? I think you'll be surprised to find that most of the time it's the woman and her demands that have caused most of her relationship problems. Now don't get me wrong: I found that it's not the woman who creates or starts the drama in the relationship, but it is the woman who gives a man chance after chance after chance to do her wrong. Then she wants to sing that you-done-me-wrong song to everyone she meets. It's time for women to wake up. It's time for women to pay attention to what they are doing. It's time for women to learn how to duck a suckah.

Women have become so accustomed to patterns, habits, and

rituals that they've forgotten how to change up those things that make them so unhappy. For me this was like an epiphany. Why don't women just stop making the same mistakes with their "partner choices"? Even more than that, why don't they just duck a suckah?

For the first time in my life I understand the kind of pain women express when they have endured bad encounters with men. The pain can come from outside forces that try to come into your relationships to destroy it or disrupt the flow of the relationship. It can come from within your circle of friends and family and from within yourself. It could be from situations where men have played games with your emotions—pretended to care for you and left you for no reason at all.

In my earlier days I couldn't figure out why women were so quick to let men use, abuse, and misuse them. Now I can identify with the confusion they faced in not understanding what went wrong. It's so simple . . . it's the woman who refuses to let go, the woman who just can't find the strength to change her bad habits, or the woman who picks the same kind of man again and again.

How to Duck a Suckah will give you the power to make better choices and not settle for being in a committed relationship with a suckah. It will help you identify and be able to point them out before they approach you. It will enlighten you and give you added knowledge. Suckahs can come from all walks of life; they can be rich or poor. So don't try to categorize them by the things they possess.

In addition, I want to give women whose spirits have been beaten down by a bad relationship or bad situations new hope that there are many better days ahead. I want women to understand that there are different forms of being strong. Every woman does not stand tall in the same way, but you can choose to stand tall and not fall for the bull crap! All you have to do is do it.

I hope that this book will find its way into the hands of someone who needs guidance in her life, who is willing to accept and receive advice from someone with years of experience as a former pimp, player, and a hustler. I hope it will enhance and impact the lives of all women who want to avoid and duck a suckah. I want to help women of all ages to become strong and more confident, to love and believe in themselves. I want this book to help rebuild their self-esteem and help them become the women God has created them to be. I believe this book will help any woman who is serious about improving her life and committed to following the steps to change inside and out.

Who Is Boom?

I'M THE BODYGUARD FOR WOMEN'S HEARTS, NOT A SELL-OUT.

I call myself the Bodyguard for Women's Hearts because everything I am going to share with you I have learned from my years of experience running the streets. My marriage, my family, my struggles, what made me change my life, my lifestyle, the reason I made the change to live a happy and healthier life. I once heard a great saying: "You will no longer need my shoulder to cry on, but you can still use it to stand on to view your new world" after reading this book.

When guys look at me and say, "Man, you are nothing but a sellout," I agree with them to a certain degree. I usually say, "Hey, man, I appreciate that, because that is a confirmation. A confirmation of the promise God has made me. Yes, my man, you are right on point. He promised I would sell out of my books." So when they call me a "sellout," I certainly don't look at it in a negative way.

You won't know the magnitude of the changes I have made until you know something about the "Old Boom." The Old Boom was a boy who grew up with a womanizer as a father. When I was a small boy, he raised me to be like him, and I took on some of the same traits. That is why I was one of the best fools you would have ever met. I found out later in the game that my father learned these traits from his father. My bloodline had so much dirt in it and so much foolishness, I felt like I needed a blood transfusion. But everyone tried to convince me that it was "all in my head." I knew they were wrong because I felt it down in my soul. The thing that I remembered best about my father was his dropping by in my younger years to whip me for being so bad. As I grew a little older, he used me as his running partner to play with his girlfriend's kids while they were having sex in another room. Afterward, we would go back home to eat dinner with my momma.

As I matured into my adulthood, if that is what you want to call it, he taught me, "Never have one woman." He said that you have to "look at women as if they are a pair of shoes because if you have one on, you are going to feel as if you are crippled." And if one gets out of line, you have to whip her like she is a child. My father was an ignorant man, and half of my life I was ignorant because I lived by his laws. I asked him a question one day, "Why do cavemen drag their women by the hair?" He answered, "Because if you drag them by the feet, they will fill up with dirt." This fool raised me with this kind of thinking. That's why I ask you not to crucify me for what I've done, because I only learned what I was taught. As I branched out into my own world, I started following other players and womanizers, and learning each and every one of their traits, until I developed my own style of playing. That is what made me so dangerous, because I was made up of many different components of the game, with nothing standing in my way. They say, "Let your conscience be your guide." But I had no conscience, and the only thing that was guiding me was *my desires*.

I dated older women at a young age and younger women at an old age. I kept anywhere from six to ten women at a time. So when one would tell me that she was tired of me and was going to leave, it was always a pleasure and a relief. I would never do anything wrong to a woman who wanted to leave, but I would give her hell if she decided to stay. So many women wasted their valuable time thinking I would come around, not knowing at the time that was as far as I could go. No woman was safe around me, not my girlfriend's mother or her best friend. Once she entered my world, I was the wolf and she was the little lamb.

Who is the "New Boom"? He is a married family man who has learned how to talk to God and get results. They say, "Be careful what you ask God for." I asked Him for a God-like wife and family, and He gave me my soul mate and a lovely daughter. I asked Him for a little, and He gave me a lot. I asked Him for a "simple little thought," and it seems as if He gave me a brain transplant because I no longer think the same. I asked Him to help me care for others, and He replaced my heart. I asked Him to make me walk the right way, and He put pep in my step. I asked Him to help me speak to women in a positive way, and you are reading my words. So now you have it. That is why I call myself the Bodyguard for Women's Hearts. And I will live up to that title. That title is mine until the day I die! Out of all that I have done, right or wrong, there is one good thing that came out of all of this. I learned that keeping your word is one of the most important things you can learn. My word is my bond and God is my witness. Here I have given my word to you.

I was watching a TV program about boot camps for troubled teenagers. I am talking about the ones who raise all the hell in troubled neighborhoods. I am talking about little Ray Ray, and little Nuc Nuc, and the gang. They think that no one can change his life, and they are going to be gangbangers until the day they die. As soon as they got caught and had to go to a different environment, I saw them marching and saying, "Yes, sir," and making up the bed. Life does have a change for you; you just haven't witnessed it yet. Maybe it's because of those two words you never said: "can't" and "ain't." I know of one word that you can use and you'll never have to worry about a thing, and that is "Jesus." Jesus doesn't force you to do anything. He'll let you volunteer, and if you don't see Him when it is your time to go, you just bought a ticket to Hell.

IT's HARD TO FIND A MAN
WHO WILL TELL THE TRUTH.

Some men stop me and say, "You are a traitor. You are giving up all of our secrets." I just say that the reason God put me on this assignment and not you is that women hear from fools every day, and every now and then they will find a man who will tell the truth. Finding a man who tells the truth is like looking for a dinosaur. When was the last time someone found a dinosaur? I want to tell the ladies that if you are going to play the game, remove your heart and let God hold it, and when you return, you'll be able to find them both in the same place. That is when you can begin your new life.

TRUE PLAYERS DON'T MIND THIS BOOK.

One thing I have noticed is that the cool men are not mad at all for me writing this book. It bothers only the weak men, who had no game to begin with. True players don't have any problems with this, because there's plenty of game out there. A man can always think of another way to do it. On top of that, most women are not going to follow and listen to these instructions. Today you will, but right after this, it will be just like you left church. You can hear the pastor preach and shout all morning, and then you'll still go and have you an afternoon delight.

DON'T HATE THE PLAYER; HATE THE GAME.

I am sitting here working out in the gym, and it just crossed my mind that I am tired of working on this treadmill. I see the same walls and equipment every day. But if I went outside and walked, the scenery would change. I would have fresh air and could walk as far as I wanted to. If a person comes out of his or her comfort zone and quits seeing the same thing every day, and travels and meets new people, it opens up a brand-new world. You'll discover that life won't be so boring. You will automatically change some things about yourself; the way you dress, the way you wear your hair. It could change the way you talk because you will have bigger and better things to talk about. That is just another one of my crazy thoughts!

Has your thunderstorm ever turned into a bright sunshiny day? Have you ever had something bad happen to you, and after it was over it seemed like it was a message getting you ready for the good things that were about to happen to you? All of a sudden the sun is shining on your life. The next time something bad happens to you, don't focus on the bad. Think about the blessings that are coming your way. It is like the song lyrics, "I can see clearly now, the rain is gone."

I am not trying to confuse anyone, but you will hear me say "suckah" and "player." They are similar, but there are differences. Suckahs have serious relationships and cheat on their women, while players don't want serious relationships because they just want to have as many women as possible. They are both trying to play the game. What makes the game different is what you bring to the table. Just look at it like you are at your job and it is potluck day. Everyone has to bring a dish of food. Just because you have a big bowl of potato salad, that doesn't make it a meal. Once everyone else brings their food, that is when it becomes a meal. It is the same thing with a suckah and a player: they are nothing without you.

MY DARKEST SECRET.

One of the ways I can make you believe I am telling the truth is to share one of my darkest secrets with you. See, I know if I tell you this, then you should trust me the rest of this journey because I am not trying to hide behind anything. I want you to know that I never read a book in my life because I was dyslexic. I want to try to get you to trust yourself and open up to the number one person, and that person is you, and be true to yourself. So with that being said I have to open up. I'm opening myself up to millions of people. The only way to open up to yourself is to change the way you think. I let the wrong people put negative thoughts in my head at a young age, and I just never tried after that. I just kept going through life trying to hide it. When you hide something at a young age, you keep doing it all your life and you end up an old person hiding the same thing that you could have fixed in your young life. So I'm asking you today to quit hiding stuff. Let's get together and try to work on something you can fix and quit being a slave to it.

BACK WHEN I WAS CRAZY.

Folks would always say, "You are such a *bad* boy." The neighbors would run when they saw me coming because I was so big for my age. I would throw rocks at their dogs, and when they came outside to tell me to stop, then I would turn and start throwing rocks at them. When they ran in the house to get away from the rocks, then my stupid behind would take it one step too far . . . and end up breaking a window! When I broke a window I would run home to tell my momma that the neighbors were teasing me, just in case they called the police. I knew that she would believe me, like most mothers. Let that be a lesson to grown-ups to check out the problem before you take sides. I guess you could say this is one of the ways that I was labeled a bad kid. Missing a father I barely knew, crying out for a man in the house.

When there is no man in the house, you have no one to pattern yourself after; this could lead to a momma's boy or a street boy. I haven't done the statistics on this, but I am pretty sure that someone has already done research; we don't need the numbers, just look around. Let's face it; it is hard for women to raise a boy alone. I started lashing out by marking and making fun of everything that someone would say. I thought life was a joke, until I tried it on my grandmother. Everything was funny, until she beat all of my senses back into me. She almost killed me. As strange as this may sound, that beating changed my life that day. I turned into a scary little boy. I questioned myself as to which road to take. They say you reap what you sow, and that is a true statement. It seemed like everyone wanted to fight me. I was a big kid but had never been in a fight in my life. I found myself running home from school every day because of the same threats that most kids hear in their young age. These threats were, "At three o'clock, we are whipping your behind." The good part was I stayed right across the street from the school. The bad part was it was a busy intersection. I can't tell you how many times I ran across the street before the crossing guard could raise his stop sign.

If you stayed close and heard a lot of screeching and horns blowing, they were blowing at me. The threats and the chase went on for quite a while. Until one day I tried to run a different way home, and I turned the wrong corner, and there was nowhere else to go. I was faced with a brick wall and a guy chasing me with half of the school running to see who was going to win the fight. The only way out was up! So I climbed and fell off the wall and onto the guy; I knocked him out cold. By the time I stood up, the crowd had made it around the corner. The crowd had started cheering for me because they thought I'd hit him and knocked him out. It didn't take long for that news to spread all over the school. After that day, no one pushed me around. But then I started to push other people around.

I then took on the role of Bully. As you are raising your kids, please understand they need more influence than whipping. Sometimes beatings add more anger when a child is trying to find his way. They even add animosity and resentfulness. That anger has to go somewhere, and mine started with girls and ended up toward women. I noticed at an early age that most girls and women have the same traits. They listened to my voice instead of their inner voice. This usually leaves a woman powerless. Once you add a little abuse to it, she ends up helpless. I also realized that once a woman makes a mistake, and knows that she has been a fool, nine chances out of ten she becomes ashamed and tries to make sure that no one else finds out. Which taught me how to manipulate a woman's mind? Which created a monster inside of me?

PIMPING AIN'T EASY.

Someone has to do it, and believe it or not, most girls want the pimp to do it. It makes them feel whole because living in what you'd call a normal world they felt like they were in a hole with no way out and nowhere to go. With a pimp, they feel like their new world is a step up. Then you have the ones who are just curious and, as they say, curiosity kills the cat. Most of these girls have low self-esteem, come from one-parent homes, or just want to live on the wild side. One of the easiest ways to break women into selling their bodies is to start them working in a strip club, even if they start out as a waitress. They will see that the girls who are dancing are making so much money that they will trade professions.

The key is to find a dancer who is happy with the money she is making but not with her job. To convince her to come into the pimping world, you would ask her, "Why would you let everyone in the room see your naked body for a few dollars and a table dance, when you can be in private and make a few hundred dollars for every man you take on?" If you get them to fall for that and convince them that you have their back, the pimping is on.

This craft has been around a long time. Only God knows exactly how long. You will have a lot of guys claiming they invented this craft, but all of them lie so much you don't know whom to believe. You'll find one twenty years old swearing that he started it all. But how could he? He's still so young his breath smells like baby food. This is an unbelievably foolish craft that people in the game take very seriously. To be respectful, let's call the girls ladies of the night. You have to be in their world to truly understand it. And if you don't abide by the rules, you can easily come up hurt.

PIMPING RULES.

Here are some of the rules of the game you won't believe. When I was in the game, if a lady of the night ran away from her pimp and wanted to come into my world, she would have to pay me to get in, and out of respect, I would call her pimp to let him know that she was no longer with him. In pimp language, that would be called "serving him the news." But now, the new pimps are using dope to control the ladies and will kill you if you try to serve them the news. Let me share a few rules with you. One of the rules is, when a pimp comes into the room to talk to another pimp, the lady of the night has to turn her head and look the other way at all times. Because if she is caught looking, it will seem like she wants to trade pimps, and that rule is called "loose eyes." Men who buy sex are called johns. This lowers the chances of married men being caught. All johns know where to find these types of women. A lot of them can be found in storefront massage parlors.

Some pimps will go to these places to try to fool these ladies to make them think they are johns. In reality they are trying to talk them into working for them. As soon as the ladies of the night find out that they are pimps, they have to face the wall and not say a word. Because a smart mouth means they are disrespecting a pimp. If that happens, he's allowed to tell you to break yourself, which means "give me your money" because you just took up some of my time. This is not robbery; it's just pimp rules. In their world, it seems like the crazier they look, the more women they catch. I guess you are trying to figure out why he has all of that stuff on, but you end up laughing and talking and falling straight into his trap. They will talk their lady of the night into bringing new girls home to work for them. This will make the new girls wives-in-law, because the one who is already there is considered to be the wife. I know that it sounds crazy; just think how crazy it would be if you were in it.

When I was in the pimp world, and you talked a woman into working for you, you first had to break her in. My pimp partner and I had a system where I would give him $150 and drop the new girl over his house and play like he is a john wanting to buy sex. This would let me know what the girl would do under pressure. After sex, he would give her the money, and I would pick her up and she would give it all to me. She would be so excited that she passed the test for her man.

Then I taught her what undercover police do and what they look like. This prepares her for hitting the streets. I can go on and on, but I am getting embarrassed that I even played this game. Although some women of the night talked me into it, it's not something I am proud of! Plus, I had to quit because I had never seen a pimp with a good retirement plan. I have seen them play around with their lives so long they end up with an old Cadillac and looking for somewhere to stay. Every good thing must come to an end. I learned if you end it before it ends you, you'll still have strength to start a new beginning. Please don't look down on me for what you just read. I am just trying to show you as many angles as I can and how choosing the wrong man could destroy your life.

BE ALL YOU CAN BE.

I was calling myself "Mr. Facts" or "Just the Facts." Some people didn't like that because they could not handle the truth, so I began to call myself "the Bodyguard for Women's Hearts." I want to protect women's hearts so much that I am willing to bring out many secrets to do so. I remember I used to get letters in the mail and, since I didn't have an education, struggled to read them. I couldn't understand my mail, and then I'd find out that I had a few speeding tickets and a subpoena for child support, and some girlfriend telling my wife I was messing around. I don't have to worry about that drama anymore because since I've married this wife, Lauren, I have been truly faithful. This is my third marriage. Some would call it my third strike. I am out of the dating game and happily married with help from God and the commitments I made. I am new and improved and have been healed! I want to help women restore their mental health. I want them to be all that they can be and do all that they can do.

A MORE POSITIVE SIDE OF BOOM.

Over the years I have changed. People do change, you know. I no longer look at things the way I used to. I have always cared for people, but now I care even more. It seems like I have gone through hell and found my way out. I am positive, and I look forward to helping those who have gotten off track to get back on track. Things can happen in your life as a kid that you have no control over. But once you grow up, you can control those things that have gotten in your way. I don't know how it happens, but it does. God wants the latter part of your life to be better than the first part of your life. You are never too far gone for God. I guess this thing is divinely appointed. People will cross your path and they will help you get to the next level and will point you in the right direction. Somehow, things just work out. They can't help you along the way if you don't want to go. It seems like everyone wants to go to Heaven, but no one wants to die. I know people who want to be rich but don't want to leave the house. So I am asking you: What are you ready for?

Another good thing about me is that I am always trying to bring out the positive side in others. I try to help people to find their true passion, and I ask them, "What are your talents?" For example, if you like to draw, why not go to school and get a degree in this field? Or, if you are not going to do that, why not search for a job or position where you have to use your skills as an artist? What about taking some advanced art classes or graphic design courses so that you can advance your true passion? Read more magazines and articles about the arts. Learn everything you can about your gift. I see this as a gift that God has given you. You may have to work hard to perfect your gift. You may have to go out of your way and do a few things that you said you were not going to do. But make investment in yourself.

I understand that college is not for everyone, but how about trade school? Things may be a little uncomfortable for a minute, so that you can reach your fullest potential and become the person that God has created you to be. Never stop trying to perfect your talent. As long as we are here on this earth, we are going to be learning something. So you might as well excel on the things that you are good at or have a passion for.

What do you have in your hands? I don't think a lot of people really think about it. Sometimes there are so many things that we are good at. But what do you like the most? You may be a good writer and an excellent bookkeeper. Along with that you may have some modeling skills. You may even be good at building things. All of that is good because it shows your versatility and ambition. What you have to do is find the one talent that holds your interest more than the other talents. There has to be one that overpowers the others. This doesn't limit you. But what it will do is allow you to focus on your gift, and then the other talents become hobbies. And when you are not using your gift, you can enjoy working on your hobbies. That way, you'll never have a dull moment in life. Your life will be full of energy and joy.

Ladies, I need you all to work with me and be on my side, like I'm on yours. I'm putting myself in harm's way. I'm standing in front of the bullet for you all. So keep me living, so that I can keep giving. One might ask, "Are you nervous?" At this point in time I would have to say yes. It's hard not to be nervous when you tell the truth about something you have done, when you know it is wrong.

Two

The Suckah

I KNOW HOW THE SUCKAH THINKS.

I really want to let women know the reason I can inform them on suckahs is that I lived half my life being a suckah. I learned how to be a cool player suckah. I have abused women and others to no end. And I want women to know that if a man strikes you or mentally abuses you, at that point you should be thinking that he needs some help. Not only does he need help, you do, too. Quit worrying about helping him and worry about yourself at this point. Get out of this mess and go and get help. I mean professional help. Get out of the sitting duck syndrome before you quack up.

THE MONSTER INSIDE ME.

What made the monster even more vicious is when I watched my sister date hoodlums. Back in the day that is what they were called. They were cool guys you did not want to cross. They would break into stores, rob people on the streets, and I was there to witness some of these crimes. Since they were older, they said that they would teach me how to be a man, since no one else took the time to do it. At that time, I was finally a young boy feeling like a man. I was so confused when I saw them murder two men on two different occasions. Even though they were teaching me this, I thought to myself this couldn't be right. They were caught and received forty years to life, and I knew that jail wasn't where I wanted to be. This left me thinking that there was no one there for me.

I grew up on the streets watching people in bad relationships. I even witnessed a woman kill her husband. I thought to myself, "Wow, dying is not much of a living." And you would think that seeing something like this would change my life and the way I treated women. It backfired, and the monster in me said, "If a woman ever shot me and didn't kill me, I would kill her." That lets you know how stupid I was. I am trying to get you to understand where kids are at in their mind, with a fast-moving world and constant pressure. It is enough to make your mind explode. I am pretty sure that you have thought of some silly thoughts too, but I am sure that you have forgotten them.

Maybe that is why when people are introduced to drugs, they get hooked because drugs take them to another place and time. Doing drugs help you to forget how cold this world really is, until you get hooked, and then your memory comes back. Like the song says, "Nobody wants you when you're down and out." Most addictions start with people saying, "It won't happen to me," but if you are doing drugs, it has already begun to take place. And then when you add sex to your addiction, now you have two things you can't stop. You can add your child's name on the world's most famous list called "a problem child." How I survived all of this only God knows! One of my biggest addictions that kept putting pressure on me was the womanizing and control addiction. In my past I dated many women. Some of them got away from me without being abused in some shape or form. I believe that I was saved for a reason. For all the lives that I ruined, I could have been dead.

I did meet plenty of good women in my life. They were just

up against a no-good man with a good heart but just didn't know what to do with it. At some point I thought, "If I get married, it will take me out of this jungle." So I picked what one would call a "nice girl," a preacher's kid. I know you are saying that don't mean a thing. But it was enough to fool me because at that point in my life I didn't know what a "good girl" was. I thought a good girl was someone who did what I told her to do. I put her in a house and car, and it seemed like everything was going fine.

But this is the mistake of a suckah who's tired of the game and doesn't know how to stop. A tired-of-the-game suckah will find a good woman, put her in wife mode, have kids, and think that now this is a family. This type of suckah will give her the credit card, the checkbook, and trust her with all of his possessions. But still, you can't trust him. Because he always wants to keep a "chick" on the side, until he gets caught. Then he'll swear it will never happen again, and you will forgive him, until you catch him in the act again. After the second time, or maybe the third time the tables will turn. You will start thinking, "What have I gotten myself into?" You will try to find your way out. The biggest mistake that most women make once they get out is leaving their hearts open, which leads into an open door back into your life. Just remember one thing: some suckahs never change!

TAKE TIME TO LEARN WHO YOU ARE.

Here's one thing I know for a fact: If men would take their time and learn who the women are they are lusting over and quit going by how wide their behind is or how nice their legs are or what they look like in their clothes, and find out who he really is, then the X's on their headboard would be fewer, because they wouldn't want to mess with half of you women. And that will give the rest of the ladies who are really trying to be outstanding beautiful people a better chance with a good man. But we are too busy looking on the outside. All that looks good isn't good.

So we continue to play the game and catch you. Then in the end we find out we really didn't want you. If we learned who you are before we started, before we even got involved with each other, half of that foolishness could be pushed to the side. It will let you understand things in a clearer way, to go on about your business. I don't know if that makes sense to you, but it usually doesn't until after the pain. Here is a pretty bold statement: A handful of you women know you are not what you claim to be. It might be more, but that is another story. But I don't have to point fingers because you know who you are. You are messing it up for the women who are about something and doing things with their life to make it beautiful.

WHERE ARE THE SUCKAHS?

I do believe that I need to start off by making you understand where the suckahs are, so that you can easily find them. You can find them all day, every day, and any given time of the day, wherever you may be. Women need to understand where suckahs hang out.

Let's start with the one who could possibly be in your home (daddy or stepdaddy), which could be the one your momma picked. Sometimes, that is where suckahism lies. I know you are saying this is not a word, but it will do! You know what I'm talking about.

Some of you have great fathers, and some of you have fathers you wish were dead. Some of you can't wait until you grow up to get out of the house to get away from the suckah. And sometimes the suckah goes beyond the call of duty and tries to add you along with the momma, like you come with the package, wrapped up in his arms, with a big bow attached. In other words, it is called child molestation. It could go as far as being your own brother.

WHAT DOES A SUCKAH LOOK LIKE?

He looks like the preacher who feeds you the Word of God on Sundays, and away from the church, he feeds you jive. There is no particular look. He could be the boy who sacks your groceries, even the guy who drives the bus that carries your children to school. He can even look like your grandfather, the one whom everyone trusts because they think he is too old to do anything. Suckahs just appear and start ruining your life. Be wise and never doubt your first thought, because that is the one God has given you.

TO A SUCKAH, THE WAY YOU LOOK MAKES A DIFFERENCE.

Believe it or not, ladies, the way you look and what you wear have a lot to do with what happens to you and what happens for you. Because, a victimizer will look at you as a victim, and if you're standing with your shoulders hunched over, there are different things about you that a man will see and let you know. He'll be able to look at you and know that you're not confident in yourself. He can attack you at any time. It also lets a man know that he can pretty much hit on you for a one-night stand and anything else he desires. When I watch programs about animals, they show that the strong always attack the weak.

DON'T SEND OUT THE WRONG VIBES.

I heard a quote the other day: There is no need in buying a whole pig to get a little sausage. Same as, Why buy the cow when you can get the milk free? Here is a rule to go by, ladies: If you think that you are ugly, somebody else might think that you are fine. As long as you think and say that you are ugly, you'll send out bad vibes. People might not want to get close to you and find out who you are and what you are about. Or there may be some suckah who will use this as a means to use you. You have set the stage to be played. He doesn't even have to work for it. You give him the permission with your vibes, the wrong vibes.

PAY ATTENTION.

Let's face it, y'all, when those guys are there trying to talk to you and ruin your life, they don't have a Ph.D. or a degree on ruining your life, so I figured we'll be even. I know what they know, and I share it with you, so you won't bring a knife to the gunfight. So if I give you the knowledge that they have, you'll be even. Now everyone will have a weapon, but you'll have an equalizer. It won't cost anything; all you have to pay is attention and be confident enough to use the weapon right away; to use the information I'm going to give you.

THE SUCKAHS' CLUB.

In order to be a member of this elite club you have to have a lot of game. And you have to be able to play the game. You have to be slick, in a sense. You must have a lot of persuasion. Persuasion becomes your best friend because you use it minute by minute and second by second. You have to make your victims believe that you can do anything and that what you are saying is the die-hard truth. You have to have good eye coordination skills—the ability to look a person in the eye and not blink. In the suckahs' club, a man must learn how to cry because some women love that type of thing. If you are a man who can cry, you have just won the heart of your victim. You must be able to drop to your knees at the drop of a hat when you want to prove something.

Some women really like this. They think a suckah is real when he pulls all of his tricks out of the basket. When you are ever in doubt about him, ask him a simple question, "Will you bring your paycheck home to me?" If he answers yes, just wait and see if he can perform that simple task. Make sure that when he gives it to you, he is not turning around and asking you for it. See if he can let you handle the bills for a while, at least six months.

Another thing a good suckah has to be is convincing enough to bring you out of your comfort zone so that you can believe him. Not every woman believes every man. There are some women for whom a man has to perform a show-and-tell show before they can believe him. They have to do a few things right to show that woman that they are worth their weight in gold. That type of woman may sit back and say in her mind, "I'll see if he does this or that." She is going to give you a certain amount of time to mess up because she doesn't fully trust you anyway. So if you are on a time schedule and mess up during that time, you are automatically out the door. She will not reveal the time schedule to anyone who knows this suckah. But, geez, if he's able to keep to that time schedule, he has hit a home run. She will brag on him and do whatever it is that he wants her to do. He will be the king and she will be the princess. He can do no wrong. She'll even give him control of the checking account.

A woman has to remember that a relationship is give and take. She has to make sure that she is not doing all the giving. This is definitely a big sign to watch for. A lot of suckahs are takers, and they are not going to give you too much of nothing, so look out for one of these big flaws. This flaw will often stare a woman in the face. You have to think that suckahs are looking out for themselves and what they can get out of someone else. They are not going to be on the losing end of any trick. They would try to fool their own mother if they could. But a lot of mothers know their children. They hear what you say, but deep down they know who you are and what you are capable of.

Another prerequisite for the suckahs' club is the ability to communicate effectively. A suckah must have the ability to make you believe that the lie he tells is the truth. You have heard the phrase "stretching the truth." A suckah will know what that means in the truest form, because he has to be able to switch roles at any time in the game. Being able to switch roles will allow him to change his story in a heartbeat. If the suckah does not stumble or repeat his words, he stands a better chance of people believing what he says. A suckah has to be able to switch his games at any time. Even if a person suspects that something is wrong, he has to come back with even stronger words so that he won't be found out. A person might ask, "How long can a suckah play this game?" My response to that is, Forever if he can. He'll walk away with a huge bank account if he is never found out. It's hard to fool a wise person, and women need to be wise.

A wise person will check things out. A wise person will get facts and case studies. She will want to know about a person's history and where he comes from. She will want to know the number of marriages the suckah has had and how many children he has. A wise person will want to know about the child support and if he pays on time. She will want to know that each child is being taken care of. You might say, "Why would she want to know all of that information?" Because this says something about the person's responsibility. And if he is taking care of his business and he has children by you, more than likely yours will be taken care of as well. So please remember that wise people think ahead.

It is hard for wise people to trust others, so a suckah would have to win your trust first. You might get over on a wise woman once, but I doubt if you will do it twice. A wise person is thinking of the future and does not want to put all her eggs in one basket. She is investing and thinking of what she is going to have when she gets old. She wants to build and is always thinking of new ways to broaden her horizons. Remember the old proverb: A wise man will change, but a fool never will.

THE PREACHER-TYPE SUCKAH.

This is a type of suckah who will go to church with you and shout hallelujah to the Most High. He will attend all of your social events with you. He will join the choir to make you think he really has it going on. If your child is in trouble at school, he'll even go to the principal's office with you for the consultation. He is very immaculate in his dressing. He's so intelligent that he could fool God's elect, if it were possible. He doesn't complain a lot, because deep in his heart he knows that he is going to do whatever he wants to anyway. This type of suckah loves to have his woman at home doing the laundry and making lunches for the next day. He praises his wife because he knows that she is "all about family." She has so much to do around the house that she doesn't have time for extra friendships and conversations. This type of suckah seems to be so in tune with you that he seems to know where every ache and pain is. But watch out! He is all about the game.

This preacher-type suckah will be after your girlfriends and your oldest daughter. He'll be so sweet that you are thinking, "Sally Jean needs help with this, and Mary Sue needs a man to help her put her bed together." He won't have to ask you if he can do it; you'll automatically send him over there because he is so sweet. You know that your friends have had a hard time all of their lives and you want them to experience what it is like to have a nice man in their lives, even if the man is your man. Of course, you are not thinking that some "stinking thinking" is going to be going on. And you certainly don't think that they are going to become his girls. But he will ease on in there and fix the items that need to be fixed, and then he'll be in there trying to fix their wounded souls.

And before you know it, Sally Jean and Mary Sue have so many things to fix that you began to wonder, "Why are they calling him so much?" not thinking that he is preparing other things as well, things that a hammer and nail cannot repair. He's preparing things with the touch of his hands and the tips of his fingers. Every time you see your friends, they are smiling, thanking you so much for your love and concern. Because if it had not been for you, things would not be as pleasurable as they are now. Look what they have gained by knowing you. You are the best thing that ever happened to them, and he is the greatest thing you have bought into their lives.

Another thing that this type of suckah will do is go and visit the elderly. He loves to make their day. All he has to do is hear of someone entering the hospital or nursing home, and he'll run right over there. You will think that he is heaven-sent. And, in all sincerity, he really does care about people, but he has some deep issues that he has not worked through, and he uses whatever escape mechanism he can to get the job done. He wants to be real, but he knows he can't be. After he has done the Lord's will by caring for the sick and shut-in, he goes and cares for those who are in need sexually. He feels fulfilled in both ways. He has done the Master's will and he has done his own will. He comes home fully satisfied and ready to work for you, because he is on fire! And you are thinking, "What kind of man do I have? Not only does he love me, but he loves the Lord just the same."

THE CONTROLLING SUCKAH.

This type of suckah has to control everything. He even chooses the friends you can hang out with. He finds something wrong with everyone but himself. He makes you think that other people are evil. He puts things in your ears that you have never even thought of. He wants to distance you from your family, so he lets you see all of their flaws. Although you already know that they are there, he makes you think that you have never thought of them before. He doesn't want your own mother to care for you, and he starts whispering little things like, "Look how your mother treats the baby girl. She treats her different than she does you." He'll even make you think that your mother loves her other children and doesn't care anything about you. You become so disoriented that you are now wondering how all of this happened and where it came from. All of a sudden, you are in the valley of decisions, because you didn't see all of this before.

THE JEALOUS SUCKAH.

Let's talk about the jealous-hearted suckah. Jealousy will get you nowhere. He is always throwing important and famous people's names around to try to make himself look good. He is always in somebody else's business. Even if you told him some dirt, he would turn it around and swear to God that he was the one who told you. He is not only a jealous-hearted suckah but a lying one too.

I want to touch on this subject deeply, because there are so many roads we can go down. Jealousy has destroyed the lives of many people, especially women. Look around at your girlfriends. How do they respond to this evilness? How do they feel about it? And how do you feel about it? Do you deal with it on a day-to-day basis, or does it pop up every now and then? Whichever case it may be, it must be looked at in a serious manner. You might be in a good relationship, but if you let jealousy creep in, it will kill the relationship. Let's wise up, ladies! Jealousy is just trifling and mean-spirited, and some of you women have it really bad. Some of you are jealous of other women you see and even of your siblings and other female relatives. You will say, "She thinks she is something because she has married a man who plays football." And you will start wishing hateful things on the person, like wishing her husband cheated on her and hurt her. You are wishing something bad will happen in someone else's life only because there is nothing good happening in your life.

THE LONG-DISTANCE SUCKAH.

A man who holds a conversation with you at his own time can lie and tell you that he's a business owner, but he is really full of cow manure. This suckah could be married and working on his third child and tell you that he is the loneliest man in the world. He would lie and tell you that he can't see you because his mother is dying and she is lying in the bed just waiting on time. Once he gets you in the mode of feeling sorry for him, he will go in for the kill and ask you to loan him some money. And once you make that mistake, it will feel like you are paying for a car you cannot drive. If and when you get to see him, it would make you want to have sex right away so you feel like you have to get something out of the deal. And you are thinking of that high phone bill! I've been a long-distance Suckah in the past with several relationships in town and one out of town. My experience of a long-distance relationship left me with plenty of time on my hands. I really think that this kind of relationship is designed for women who don't want to be married and want an every-now-and-then man. To avoid getting hurt by this suckah, never move to his environment. Let him move to yours, so if you ever need to put him out, you still have a home.

BEWARE OF STRANGER DANGER.

Always approach every man like a stranger danger. There's danger in every stranger until you find out what he wants from you. You send your babies off to college to run into young suckahs. You see, once you send your daughters off to college, that's like sending them to a nightclub these days. They are free. They are there with the cute little boys. It seems like no one is there to get lessons anymore. It's about fun. They don't have to ask nobody anything. So I'm telling you ladies, if you are reading this book and you have a niece, a daughter, a cousin, or any young lady around you, then you need to share this book with her or give her her own copy. You have to because she doesn't know. Most girls go by what they hear and what they see. If they are hearing some mess, they'll fall for it because that is the way it goes.

If the powerful suckahs come to you with gifts, money, and dazzle and distract you, the regular suckahs will just try to use words and kindness. I think that the worst thing that can happen to a woman is to get sucked up in a suckah's way of life and have nowhere to go, no way out. That's how he traps you. You become comfortable and live just to live and don't apply anything to your life like saving money, having friends, and going places with your kids. And even when things start getting uncomfortable, you still stay in that uncomfortable zone. To avoid the stranger, keep doing things for yourself.

THE MIDNIGHT STAR SUCKAH.

A midnight star—every woman knows one of these suckahs. He is the one who will worry you to death, but you know not to date him because you don't want anyone to know he is a suckah with a face that only his mother can love. I am talking about so rough looking that you can't look him in the eye. You often thought about giving him a chance, but you can't bring yourself to do this because if you take a gorilla home after dark, he might surprise you, and you'll want to be seen with him in the light. This is a suckah who, when he gets with you, knows it's a miracle. So he has to prove himself in the bedroom. This man has more moves than Jell-O. He'll make you leave work early and tell your boss, "I won't be at work tomorrow." Not because you'll feel bad, but because you'll feel so good.

This suckah will do things to you that a monkey can't do to a coconut. About thirty days into this situation, you'll find yourself smiling and walking down the street with him waving at all your friends. It will make you finally understand that you can't judge a book by its cover. I wanted to hide this secret from you because I wanted you to finish reading this book. I knew that as soon as I convinced you that this was okay, you would throw this book down and go and dig for that ugly man's phone number that you have laid to the side, just in case. P.S. Be careful when he asks you to have his baby.

THE CROSS-DRESSING SUCKAH.

It is not a good feeling to come home and find your man sitting up with your drawers jammed up in the crack of his behind. He is so caught up with what he is doing that he didn't hear you coming through the door. Now that he has looked up and seen you looking at him, he dives for the bathroom door and knocks over your good lamp while trying to run away. You go to your closet to find out what else is missing.

You notice that the back of a pair of your shoes is bent where he has tried to jam his big foot in your shoe. And you look around and see all your bras on the floor, like he has been searching for the right one to fit his big wide back. Why in hell is your lipstick worn down to the handle? You are thinking that if he would spend as much time trying to be a man as he is trying to be a woman, you just might have something. I'm begging you, don't kill him; just put him out in the pasture with those other fools. Straighten your closet back up and keep working on yourself, because if you accept him as your man, you'll have plenty of work to do.

THE SCARED SUCKAH.

A scared suckah is the type of man who will roar like a lion when he is telling you what he will do to somebody. But when it is time for action, he acts like a kitty cat. You can't even walk down the street with this type of man without him getting on your nerves. He is telling you to cross to the other side of the street because he sees four teenagers standing in a circle talking and they might be part of a gang. So you go along with it, but then he wants to cross back over four blocks down the street, because "that dog is loose down there, he might bite." This is the type of man who will buy a dog to put in the yard so that the dog can bark and let him know that there is something going on outside. Now every time he hears the dog barking, he runs out on the front porch and fires his gun in the air, saying, "All right now, I will kill you." Because he has fired the gun so many times, the SWAT team surrounds your house. Now they are making you come out of the house with your hands up too.

The Suckah with Big Dreams
and Little Money.

This is the type of man who always has a big idea and no way to fund it. He has champagne ideas with soda pop money. His angle is to seek a women with a good job and a nice savings account, even good credit. His job is to drain every penny he can from you to make his dream come true. The only way he can do that is to swear to God that he loves you and worships the ground you walk on. That is the only way he can set you up. It is what we call fattening up the frog to feed the snake. It always seems like your money is never enough. He goes as far as having you borrow money from your mother, or even your friends. He looks in your kids' rooms at their piggy bank. He never accomplishes his dreams.

Once you catch him messing around with another woman, he'll swear it is for the money so that he can finish his project, so that his project will help you both reach your financial goals and independence. He would make you believe that he is doing this for both of you. You will go around telling your girlfriends the story of how he is using her to take care of us. You haven't realized it yet, but you didn't need her money before this game started. This story ends up with two broke women and a man who has moved on.

The No Satisfaction Suckah.

This is a suckah who brags about how good he is in bed no matter where he is. He'll be lying on the beach and brag about it. This is your anyplace, anytime, and anywhere type of man. This is the man who can talk you into a one-night stand. And when he finishes making love to you, you won't understand how you fell for something that he couldn't do. This is a man who usually gets sent home before he finishes the job. It won't take you long to realize that he is all talk. He'll leave you wondering when he is going to start, but he's already finished. You will begin to realize why his friends call him the minute man. I know you have heard of show-and-tell. But he is a man with a tall tale and no show. You can tell who he is. He's long on conversation and short on performance. But you gave him the benefit of the doubt and you are still in heat and have to do without.

THE DOWN-LOW MAN, THE WORST
SUCKAH OF THEM ALL.

The down-low man is the worst because he has you and a boyfriend. You are talking about evil spirits, Lord, have mercy! And you don't even know it. Now you are loving him when he has been loving on some other man. And that, ladies, is a crying shame.

If your man has a tattoo on his behind, he's questionable. I am not going to sit there long enough for a man to hold my behind and stick a needle in to draw a picture. I'm sorry; this is just my opinion. So if your man walks around with your name tattooed on his behind, if you like it, then I love it. But to me, it is questionable.

If your man likes wearing women's undergarments or underwear because it's comfortable, he's questionable. I would really do some research on him. In my world, that is not right. Now I don't know about this new world. I guess with these new guys, maybe they think it's right. I have worn some drawers so long that they start shining like silk. Oh, and I have had some drawers that were too small and ended up in me like a G-string. I have even worn some drawers so long just the seams of the drawers were on me. Yet even with all my bad drawer experiences, I still am not going to put on women's underwear.

A Suckah Will Lie When the Truth Will Do.

Let me tell you about another suckah—a lying suckah. That's a piece of work right there. I'm pretty sure all of you know of someone who lost a home or something of great value because he lied. What causes these things? Is it because they want their cake and want to eat it too? Is that it? Or do they think they are just going to get away with it? What is it? Really, what we have here, ladies, is a case of mistaken identity. Once you think you know your man enough to start loving him, you forget to keep checking to see if he loves you. This is what happens to most women. They are so happy to find someone to love that they give all they have but end up forgetting about themselves. They gain weight and forget their upkeep. Their health begins to decline. All of these things make the exit for men a little easier to do. That is why when the relationship is over, the woman plays the fool, because it is so hard to take all of you back.

The Stuck Duck.

You and your family are arguing because they told you the man wasn't any good and you went against their word and ran your behind over there, trying to get the better things in life (you thought). See, sometimes people from the outside can see things better because they have nothing invested. You are so invested in this thing with him that you can't see straight. You are so busy trying to love or get something from the situation that you lose yourself. Now you are stuck! You are stuck on stupid. You don't have anywhere to go. You might get a present here and there, you might get to fly a few times, but really you are miserable.

IT'S BETTER TO BE THE ONE WHO GOT AWAY THAN THE ONE WHO GOT CAUGHT.

Let's look at it like fishing. When you are a fisherman like most men, it is the sport of the game. It's not eating the fish that's exciting; it's catching the fish that brings total fulfillment. So what happens when you eat so much fish that you get tired of eating it? What do you do? Do you give it away? Or do you say, "Man, do you eat fish, do you want these?" That's what you become, a fish. You become a fish that gets passed on, or they'll take you off the hook and throw you back in the water and try to catch one better or bigger. If you are the one who got away, a man will talk about it for the rest of his life. He will tell his friends how he went fishing but she got away. He will tell them, "I almost had it." We'll talk about the fish we almost had and how she got away for a lifetime. The ones we catch, there is no need to talk about them, because the story is over anyway.

ALL MEN ARE NOT DOGS.

This is a hard one for me. Sometimes you really do have a good man. All men are not dogs. There are some men who have finally grown up and wish they could be blessed with a good woman. And all women are thinking is that all men are playing around and not serious and he don't want you. Your friends will say, "Girl, he's probably married." He probably is, or probably isn't. Well, probably is not good enough. You cannot go by what your girlfriends said. "Probably and almost" never won a trophy or a contest. It is best to just say, "Peace, be still," and look around a lot, listen, and get a feel of the spirit that is coming from this guy and know what he is trying to put in your heart. And then you will be able to evaluate the seriousness of the person and see if he is playing or not. Of course, we all play games, but guess what? You play games too. So at some point, if you become serious with yourself, the playing will stop. Maybe you are suffering from the I-don't-trust-nobody disease.

I Want to Help Women Help Themselves.

A partner of mine likes to say, "Women always say men are dogs, but there are some kitty cats running that street too." And that's a true saying. Some women have men at home watching the kids while they are running the streets. So really, all the stuff I'm saying in this book goes for men and women. There are some suckah women too. That is another book. But right now I ask God to help me help women. Although this book is for women about men, sometimes I have to tell you about a no-good woman to help you understand life. I could write a book for men and it would be awfully juicy because some of you women are off the chain, and because you have been hurt, you refuse to let someone else run over you, so you think you can just have sex with men and that's it.

THREE

Men and Women Are Different

There's a book called *Men Are from Mars, Women Are from Venus*. I agree that men and women do think differently. To show you an example of what I mean, look at this: Men see two ones and they will think of the number eleven (11). Women see two ones and they will think of the number two (2). But nobody told you to add that. There's no plus sign there. But women are always trying to do something extra, and then when it don't work out they'll run somewhere asking someone what to do.

IS IT AS SIMPLE AS MEN AND WOMEN BEING DIFFERENT?

Some might say that men are like horses and women are cows, but you know what? They both eat hay. Forget that women and men are different, because people in general are just different. This is why when you go to join hands with someone, you have to be equally yoked. Even then, though, you'll still have your problems. At times you may even feel like you have picked a rotten egg. But God bless you if you don't get with someone who is at least your spiritual equal, 'cause you are going to need it.

You Gotta Let Your Man Be a Man.

I really don't know how to explain this, but if you are a controlling lady and you think you got the ups on your man 'cause you can tell him what to do, you are missing out on something good. Until you let your man be a man, he'll never be a man for you. Now, I know I said this before, but the way to bring out the man in your man is for you to be more of a woman. I guess you can consider him a weak suckah but a good man!

Stop Dragging Your Man Around by the Hand.

Here is some advice: Ladies, stop dragging your man around by his hand. Girls follow, men lead. Girls are not supposed to be in the front. Grab his hand and let him lead you. You cannot wear the pants and be the buffalo soldier in the house. You have to ask yourself what kind of man you want. What kind of man do you expect your man to be? What kind of man do you think he can be when you try to act tough like a man?

Let's Bring Chivalry Back.

If you go out on the street, especially on the sidewalk, get your behind on the opposite side of the traffic. He is always supposed to be on the side where the traffic is, so that if a car comes and jumps over the curb, he will take the lick, not you. Stop getting in the car at the same time he does—wait on him to open the car door for you. I think all you women know this, but men really don't do that anymore. I suggest you sit there until he does. The first time my wife tried it, I almost drove off. I didn't even know she wasn't in the car because I wasn't used to that. I have learned a few things since then. Now, our lives are so busy that we agreed I can open the door for her at church and when we go to special events. Besides, I don't want someone to wreck the back of the car in a busy parking lot while I'm trying to be a gentleman. When you are sitting in a restaurant, always let your man sit where he can watch the door, just in case some crazy fool comes in. You won't have to scream, "Oh, my God!" He'll already know what's going on and be ready to protect you. Let's face it, you won't do anything but hide, anyway.

Let Your Man Handle the Man Situations.

Here's another rule to let your man be a man. If someone has done something wrong to you, or said something wrong to you, and your man steps up to find out what the problem is, calm down and let him handle that in a manly way. We don't need that extra behind-the-scenes talking, because you are the one who got this mess started, anyway. Stay out of a man's way when he is taking care of business.

Are You the Head or the Tail?

You know I want to talk to the ladies about men being the "head of the household." Sometimes it seems like they are trying to take control of you and make you do something you don't want to do, but the man was put in a position to be over you for a reason. He is really trying to protect you. Like I ask my wife, "Baby, where are you?" It is late at night and she is riding around with her top down on her car, and it is dangerous out there, especially nowadays. Sometimes she thinks that I am trying to make her come home, but really I'm just trying to make sure she's home because I can protect her in our home. I definitely want her to enjoy her freedom, but I also know that everyone does not think like that, and she may run across someone evil who may try to attack her.

So quit thinking that men are always trying to control you, because they may just want you in a safe place. Men know that the shopping mall is closing in ten minutes and want you home although you haven't found the right dress. We know that you want to shop until you drop and are not thinking about your safety. You have a man at home who wants you to return to him in one piece, not torn up, bruised, and raggedy.

DON'T ACT LIKE YOU HAVE MORE THAN HIM.

If you meet a good man you like, and you start out with more than he has, don't act like it. Don't be talking about "all this is mine." How about, "If we become one, what's mine is yours." If you take his manhood away, you'll end up with half a man. Just keep supporting your man, planning your future, working together, praying together for blessings to overtake you-all once you start working together.

THE ONLY GOOD MAN IS A GOOD MAN.

I think we are at the point where we have to change some of these old sayings. For the new generation, they don't make sense. For example, "The only good man is a dead man." I beg to differ with that. I'm a good man and I am alive. I think we should change the saying to. "The only good man is a good man."

FOUR

Appearance

SEVEN IMPORTANT BEAUTY BASICS STEPS MY WIFE USES.

1. Establish an intelligent and well-balanced daily diet, including foods rich in vitamin A.
2. Work toward a relaxed, tension-free approach to living.
3. Maintain a sufficient daily water intake: six to eight glasses daily.
4. Maintain good elimination habits.
5. Get sufficient rest (eight hours of sleep nightly is the norm).
6. Exercise daily.
7. Get regular facials. This helps stimulate the blood flow to the face. Without a healthy blood supply, your skin cannot be healthy.

HOW AN UPGRADE SUCKAH PLAYS FOR KEEPS.

When an upgrade suckah approaches a diva, he already recognizes how much it costs to help keep you. This is when the show starts; he will use every trick in the book. He will start by showing you all the material things. Should you entertain this? Maybe—as long as you are in control.

One day, he may ask you to marry him. Now you are his trophy wife. Men are always looking for that special "trophy" one might call a diva. Here are some of the traits of a diva: a perfect posture that gives the appearance of confidence and poise. Like your mother always says, sit up straight! Body alignment gives a more youthful appearance: Stop walking hunched over like your stomach hurts. Place one foot in front of the other and act like a runway model. If it sounds like too much work to you, that's why every woman cannot be a diva.

DON'T WEAR YOUR CLOTHES TOO TIGHT.

Here is a new rule: If you can pinch a handful of meat standing up, then how much of it do you think will hang out when you sit your butt down? You know that doesn't make any sense. Just because you see somebody else doing it doesn't mean you have to do it. And if you are her girlfriend and let her leave the house like that, then you need your behind whipped.

ACT LIKE A DIVA.

I don't care if you've been poor all your life and live in the projects, drive a raggedy little car, and work at a low-paying job. At least you're working and making a decent living. Regardless of economic background, women need love and a committed long-lasting relationship. Ladies, just know and remember that high-income men go everywhere. Maybe you're working at a burger joint and he walks in to grab a burger. He could look over the counter and say, "Wow, that lady is pretty nice." He could ask for your phone number. He could call and you-all start dating. This could happen. It's happened plenty of times. But you can't expect that ever to happen if you act like a gangster, stuck up, insensitive, snobbish, and playing hard to get. You don't have to play hard to get; just make your body hard to get and be a lady at all times. You can't drive his Range Rover or Rolls-Royce leaning like some brother. Straighten up, be a diva. Take out all of those different-color hairpieces in your hair. Go Halle Berry on men's behinds. Remember, a businessman will never take a gangsterlike woman to a business event.

MAKE THE EXTRA EFFORT.

Make yourself presentable enough when you go out in case Mr. Right or Mr. Equally Yoked is out there looking to catch himself a woman. Put on something nice and quit saying, "I want to be comfortable." Sometimes, you have to be uncomfortable to find yourself in a comfortable situation. You can be comfortable later, once the right man finds you. I'm sure you have a dress in your closet you're saving for a special occasion. Today is the day to put it on. Take off that dingy jogging suit, get up and go in your closet, and work your magic.

A PRETTY YARD DOESN'T MEAN A HOUSE IS IN ORDER.

You may think that having a beautiful car and a beautiful home will put you above everyone else. Just because someone's yard is pretty doesn't mean her house is in order. Stop trying to keep up with the Joneses. Clean up your own backyard and stop looking over your neighbor's fence.

IF YOU'RE A DIRTY WOMAN LIVING IN YOUR HOUSE, IN HIS MIND YOU'LL BE A DIRTY WOMAN IN HIS HOUSE.

When a man comes into your home and it's not clean, he'll think you're nasty. He'll think, "Hey, this is going to be a problem because if she's not cleaning her stuff up, she surely will not be cleaning mine." Right there, it may stop you from getting a good man. Something that simple! Besides, an orderly house is a sign of an orderly mind.

KEEP YOUR UNDERWEAR CLEAN
AND IN GOOD SHAPE.

This is really important. Thought I'd mention it. Nice, clean, and matching underwear daily. Don't match them just because you think something's going to happen; it really makes a difference in the way you think, look, and feel about yourself. You don't want to wear clothes that men can see through to the type of underwear you have on. They might get the wrong impression and think that you are easy.

THE SMALLEST THINGS MAKE A DIFFERENCE.

I can't tell you how many good women I have turned down just because I didn't like something about them. She could've been the most beautiful person in the world, and I'd say, "No, man, I don't like the way her toenails look," something as stupid as that. All she needed to do was polish them. Women are guilty of the same thing. They will pass up a good man because his shoes are old and dirty, he needs grooming, and he is overweight. Or his teeth are bad and he could even have that good-Lord-have-mercy breath. They say the only time it's broke, it's when you can't fix it. Ladies, these things can be improved with a little work and coaching.

My wife is always on me about my hair. She would say, "Baby, do you think it's time to get a haircut?" I would say to her, "I have over a hundred hats. Why are you worried about my hair?" And she would reply, "The hat will not cover your neck." In my language, my kitchen was nappy! I would go get a haircut, and when she got home I would make sure she saw it. If she did not say anything about my haircut, just know that's an argument waiting to happen. Once you convince your man to do something, give him a compliment. Something as small as not complimenting him could lead him back to the land of suckahs, especially if he just left there.

DON'T LET YOURSELF GO.

If you gained a hundred and fifty pounds or seventy-five pounds and still want your man to keep complimenting you, that's not right. What if you don't ever fix it? Weight doesn't change just your body; it changes your attitude too. Your man will still love you, but it does affect things. Check your underwear size when you got with or married him. (I am quite sure you kept at least one small pair as, you say, the weight "snuck up" on you.) Compare the size you are now to them. Don't start that crying, just do something about it.

LOOKS ARE DECEIVING, EVEN MINE.

It's funny when you think somebody's built and you find that he or she is not. Take me, for example. People are like, "Man, you are so big, but you are in shape." It's because I'm holding my breath. I usually raise my shoulders back and bring my chest up, then lower my voice, "What's up, dog?" I know women are holding their gut in, sticking their butt out, and trying to make it look like they have a little shape on them. Don't act like you don't do it! We all do it! I don't even know why we do it, because once you get with the person you are going to be with, you are going to have to show your true self, anyway. Once those girdles and control-top panty hose come off, you will be under the cover trying to throw a shoe to turn the light switch off. Then you'll want to invest in a clap-off device so you won't have to leave the bed to turn the light off. My point is, if we have body issues, let's at least try to work on them instead of trying to fool each other.

FIVE

On Dating

YOU SHOULD NOT LOOK FOR A MAN.
Since you are probably going to do it anyway, when you go
out to a club, you have to remember one thing: You are on
his playing ground. He might as well say to you, "Welcome,
may I help you?" You just entered a man's world. Men are
very familiar with it. They know if it's your first time there,
or if you have been there before with the same man or a
different man. They will notice if you are just coming with
your girlfriends every time. They're watching all of that. They
are always looking to see what woman is up for the catching.
There are certain kinds of men who frequent these clubs, and
they're usually not good.

Men don't think that you are out just to dance. Maybe
you are and maybe you're not, but I think that when you are
ready to settle down, this kind of partying needs to stop. If
you start going to a milder setting, the quality of men will
change. Instead of partying in the nightclubs, why not try the
jazz clubs? The men in the jazz clubs are a little subtler. They
are in a different mode because the music is a little slower and
you can't get out there and hip-hop dance. This small change
could change your whole life.

DATING AT WORK.

I want to make a note about dating at work. You can love your work, but you can't be in love at work. It's fun when you are talking to your partner in the morning and he's telling you what you need to do, but once you have sex with him, he doesn't want you around at work and he doesn't want you telling him about all of your problems. Now you are feeling silly and stupid and either quit your job or get fired. Now you have done something crazy and your family is hungry, because you don't have a check coming in. You let someone take that away from you. You know that you were the only supporter of the family, all because you had sex with the wrong man. And you didn't know how to separate work from pleasure.

MAKING THE FIRST CALL.

Once you make the first call, you show interest and make him change his approach to pursuing you. It's much easier now, because the phone call has told him so. He could have been lining up a date to wine and dine you. That plan he had lined up has now been reduced to a drink at the coffeehouse. They say that one bad apple can spoil the whole bunch. I guess a phone call can too.

DON'T LET HIM KNOW WHERE YOU LIVE TOO SOON.

When you let a man come by your house too soon and you realize you don't want to see him anymore, it is not as easy as you think to get rid of him because he has too much information. You shouldn't have to worry that he's sitting down the street or on your steps when you get home. You shouldn't have to end up having to get a restraining order. Sometimes it could take the police two hours to get there, and we all know the system has failed many women before. So why take that chance? Always give him your cell phone number first, so that when he calls you can always be "on the run." If you give him your home number, he knows exactly where to find you. You always want to be able to have a good night's sleep.

DON'T TALK TOO MUCH.

Why would you tell him everything about you, when you know nothing about him? You might as well give him the strings to your heart so he can fly you like a kite. That is some valuable information you are giving him and you don't know the damage you are doing to yourself. It will be easier to give him the keys to your heart. Giving a man the keys to your heart too soon is like giving a thief a key to your home. When it comes to men, it is better to listen and learn than to speak and try to teach. It's like the old saying goes: If you find a fool, bump his head.

DON'T INTRODUCE HIM TO YOUR LOVED ONES TOO SOON.

Once you introduce him to your family members, they might adore him more than you do. They will always encourage you to keep him because he is putting on a show and seems like he's the nicest guy in the world. Don't fall for that trick, unless your dog likes him too. Then maybe you could be wrong; maybe your judgment is off. But you don't want your family's opinions clouding your mind.

DON'T LET HIM RUSH YOU.

When a man talks you into going to his home or his hotel room, just 'cause you walk to the door doesn't mean you have to go through the door. If you get to the door and your body is telling you yes but your mind is telling you no, then walk away from the door. Get in your car and go home. If you watch how a guy treats you on the first date, it could be a one-night stand. If he tries to get in your pants, this should tell you things you don't have to ask questions about. When you are not around, he'll meet somebody else and try to get in her pants right away too. If you meet a man who is not trying to move too early or too fast, it might be worth investigating. So please take this into consideration.

DON'T LET WHAT YOU DON'T LIKE DRAG YOU DOWN.

If you have a bad date with a man, don't let it drag you down. If you really want him, wait and see if he can come up to your level. Don't let him make you think that you are not worth anything. You have to stand firm and hold your ground, because once you give your body to him, it could be all he wants. Since I'm teaching you to think like a man, I'll use this phrase, "When it comes to your life, get in there and fight like a man." But remain a lady at all times.

DON'T GIVE YOUR HEART TOO EARLY.

One of the problems with women is they start looking for something like a fairy tale story, and when a man gives you a few words, you give him big results. Many of you know when you meet a man that he has only 10 percent of what you want. You have to realize that as soon as he does something wrong, you're going to lose 5 percent of that. You can change that. How about meeting a man who has more of what you want right off the bat and waiting for him to show you big results? Even then, give him not 100 percent but only 50 percent. Give him enough so that you have something left. Whether he breaks your heart or takes your behind out, if you don't give him all of you, then you are strong enough to use what you have left to build yourself back up. Give your whole heart to God, the man who really deserves it. You have the power to make decisions in your life. When you make a split-second decision, you can end up with a split heart.

THE CANDY STORE.

Just because I am writing a book called *How to Duck a Suckah* doesn't mean you have to avoid men. You can go into the candy store and get you a suckah if you want one. At the candy store, there are all kinds of suckers. You can find something that is suitable for your taste. Suckers comes in all shapes and sizes and colors too. Please don't limit yourself. Try different kinds of candy to see which one you like. Sometimes, a person may think that she doesn't like a certain kind until she tries it. Once you try it, you may find that you not only like it but also love it. I certainly don't mean for you to try out a man sexually. Remember my first book, *If You Want Closure in Your Relationship, Start with Your Legs*.

Try to gain strength and move on to someone who wants you in his life. If you do this, you will probably end up with a meaningful relationship. Because if a person wants you and you want him, you will try harder to make sure the relationship works. Things are much better when two people agree on a situation. People are just like suckers: They come in all sizes, shapes, and colors. If you see something you like, or something you desire, you have to try it to see if it really is something you want. You can go on a date or to a movie. Having lunch with a person you like is okay. You can even attend a concert or play with him. There are ways to test the waters before the water tests you.

Six

Sex

YOUR BODY.

If you still have sex before marriage, I have a tip for you that might keep your mind and heart attached until you get where you are trying to go. If you meet a man, and you know you are not going to be able to hold up strong, don't go to his house and don't let him come to yours. If you tell him to come over and let's have sex, he'll stop by even if he doesn't like you. Sex is free, it won't cost him a dime. He doesn't have to take you to dinner or hold a conversation with you. He just has to get in and do what he came to do. He can leave without kissing you good-bye. That's the difference between someone you date and someone you just see.

If you want to find out how a man really wants you, make him take you to a hotel, not a motel; there is a difference. A motel has continental breakfast, and a hotel has full room service. Go ahead and order you some champagne and caviar, which you'll probably end up spitting out because it's an acquired taste, but that has nothing to do with the test we are doing. We are just trying to see where he draws the line on his credit card. Always remember to make sure that someone has protection. If he doesn't, that tells you something right there. You might be messing with a nasty man.

After sex, get up and dust yourself off, and go home. Don't

ever mention how good it was. The only thing you are allowed to say is, "Thanks, I needed that, I'll see you around." Make sure you look at him on your way out the door, because you will see him pulling the cover up in the middle of his chest as if he was a woman, because you have done something that has never been done before. You are different. You have pulled the move of all moves, because men get their thrill by leaving you in the bed, wanting more.

If you handled your business right, you'll hear him say, "Please don't leave." Now, the next day you will get an early phone call from him, because he needs to hear you say, "What did you do to me, Lord have mercy, I can barely walk." Let that call go to voice mail, then around high noon, call him and say, "I am returning your call." He'll reply, "I'm just trying to see how you are feeling." Simply say, "I'm good. Are you all right?" Now tell him to call you later, because you have another call coming in.

What this does, ladies, is make him do everything in his power to have another date with you. He'll make it bigger, better, and longer the next time. Now you are getting to the investment part of the relationship. He is putting so much time and effort into you that he cannot afford to pull away, because he will lose, and we all know that manhood and losing do not match. If you just have to continue with this type of behavior, let's try one person at a time. At least you will know who the baby's daddy is or where you got the disease.

HAVING SEX TOO EARLY.

By having sex too early, you use the leverage and the understanding that you could have to make him appreciate you better. If you have already done it, you'd better hope that he likes and cares about you enough to stick around and find out about the rest of you. To most men, you've already given the best part. Just remember in the beginning, love always starts off as a game. I had a few women write me to ask how long is too long. One of them said she took it slow and waited for a month and a half. I thought I would hate to see what she would do if she was taking it fast. She would have had sex as soon as he said hi!

DON'T CONFUSE SEX WITH LOVE.

If all he wants to do is make love, you are misunderstanding the situation. When you want to go to the park and hold hands, his mind is still on going to bed and making love. When you want to go on the shopping spree he has promised you, he's buying time until he can get everything he wants out of you. He already knows that he didn't come to stay, and you will soon find out that you were just in the way.

TAKE OFF YOUR HEART ALONG WITH YOUR CLOTHES.

When you are ready to be intimate with him, you know you will throw your shirt, bra, skirt, dress, or pants on the floor. You open the condom, and even the wrapper goes on the floor. Then you just dive into bed. Tell you what, why don't you do this while you are throwing everything on the floor: Why don't you take your heart out and throw it on the floor with all the other things? If you can do this, he will be able to hurt only your behind and not your heart. I know that it's impossible to take it off physically, but mentally you are going to wish you had. Especially when you find out it was a one-night stand, and the only thing he left was a broken heart and the promises and lies he told to get you in bed. When you fall in love with a man and he is not in love with you, that is some pain. You have to make sure that person is in love with you too. Otherwise you'll end up singing that old song that says, "I found love on a two-way street and lost it on a lonely highway."

DON'T BE A RESTING PLACE.

If you let a man into your life and he comes and goes as he pleases and gets some from you every time he wants it, he may love you, but he has to go. You are just a resting place for him. You are just a place he can go to gather himself before he gets back out there and plays the game. If you are a resting place, what happens when he gets plenty of rest?

QUIT HAVING SEX FOR A WHILE.

Women say they are not going to give their heart. Your heart is not the only thing men are getting. When men get your behind, you are inviting those evil spirits in you and it is breaking your body down. You are going to look like an old, used-up woman when you do decide to have a relationship. You think you can just have sex and move on. Why not quit having sex for a while? And while you're at it, quit going to male strip clubs and giving away your hard-earned money and, for some of you, your kids' lunch money. Turn on the TV or grab your Bible. Once you see a naked body, your mind will turn to thoughts you shouldn't have. Instead, take the time to understand what your life should really be about and who you really are. The next time you have sex, it might really mean something. I sometimes like to say, "You don't realize how much of yourself you are giving when you call yourself getting." To tell you the truth, all you are doing when you have meaningless sex is bursting blood cells.

YOUR BODY GIVES LIFE
SO IT'S A NATURAL PHENOMENON.

I look at a woman's body like a well-oiled machine, because it gives life. Big factories have expensive machines that put out products.

They don't let just anybody go over there and start pushing buttons. Then why would you? You have a machine that makes life; that's you. Most men have no training, yet you allow them to work on you to see if they can get you started. You wouldn't want a plumber operating on you. You know he is going to kill you because he knows nothing about the body. So why do you think sex won't kill you? From now on, when you think about sex, repeat to yourself, "I want to live to see another day." Really, I'm not trying to stop you from having sex; I'm just trying to keep you alive.

HIV IS REAL!

You know back in my day, I use to be in love with the way strippers looked. I used to go to the strip clubs every night and chase women to get them to work for me. I really fell in love with the way this one girl carried herself and her personality. I was like, "Wow, man, I would date this girl." Instead of trying to get her to work for me, I actually was trying to make her my girlfriend. She would let me come over and cook for me and everything, but she would not have sex with me. Then one day she asked me, "What do you think about people who have AIDS?" I said, "Well, I wouldn't want to eat behind them and I wouldn't kiss them. I wouldn't mind talking to them, but it would be hard for me to touch them." She said, "Well, I just want you to know that I have AIDS." And my heart dropped down in my chest because I realized that she saved my life. I would have actually started a relationship and had unprotected sex with this girl. Greedy me was trying to push her to mess with me, not even thinking about sexually transmitted diseases. It's the same thing with all of us. We never stop to really think or smell the roses. Next time, before you bite off more than you can chew, think about that person's history.

How Many Times Have You
Been Saved from HIV?

Being a woman, men will beg you twenty-four hours for sex, because we know if you hear "sex" enough, sooner or later it will brainwash you and you will give up and give in. How many times have you said no? That could have been the one you fell for and didn't use protection with or the condom could've broken. What I want you to do now is thank God for your blessing and quit counting the days that you have not had sex. Women would say it has been three months. "Lord, I don't know what to do." Keep on counting the days and blessings.

SEVEN

Relationships

COULD BE LONELY, COULD BE NOT.
According to a *New York Times* poll, 51 percent of women in 2005 reported they lived without a spouse. Census data from that same year finds that widows and divorced women of various ages opt to not get remarried. Women seem to be happy with Mr. Right Now. Single women are taking control of their lives with or without a man. Women are just not willing to go through the emotions to find out he really isn't worth it.

Women who have been married and are now divorced or widowed seem to have the attitude that single is better. They already have their kids, money isn't an issue, and their friends are an incredible support system. For them, men are the whipped cream. It's additional calories, but it is so sweet you can do with or without it. Still, not all mature single girls are just out to have fun. Some feel, "I have enjoyed a fairly successful career but at that clock-ticking age, I would give this all up in a minute to turn the clock back and focus on my Mr. Right. But for now, I'll take Mr. Right Now."

Understand your motivation for dating Mr. Right Now. The trick is to be in control. Understand your motivations, or else risk being driven by a vast haze of subconscious needs and ideas. Ask friends you trust and who know your history for feedback about how you're conducting your dating life. This can help you sort things out.

For example, you might find yourself attracted to dating material, but you both fear the commitment, and you find yourself crying yourself to sleep alone night after night. When that moment—I do mean moment—is over, how does that add to your life? Maybe you're still holding on to that hurt, like the night you found out he was cheating. It was devastating, but maybe it's time to let it go.

Maybe you need to enter therapy to deal with your long-buried feelings of betrayal and loss. Maybe the only person you need to date is yourself. Maybe you need a man break to figure out who you are and what you want. For some women, it's a serious relationship or nothing. They tend to view every man as a potential marriage partner. They are the intense ones, so you can imagine the amount of pressure they put out. Guys run for the hills, and the women wonder why they can't get even a Mr. Right Now.

Some women who date Mr. Right Now could love the idea of being a mistress to an unmarried man—you see each other just a few days a week so it never gets stale. It also allows them to keep themselves in an attachment-free emotional state; it's healthier and less off-putting than the former must-marry syndrome. You can still in your heart of hearts long for intimacy.

CAN THERE BE A HAPPY MEDIUM?

Even if your agenda is ultimately to find the one, having a casual, nonjudgmental attitude toward men allows you to lower your expectations and thus suffer fewer disappointments. And you're more appealing than when you clutch in desperation. Plus, your date can be more enjoyable if you are not upset about the future. You must find a balance.

A woman who is willing to date Mr. Right Now and enjoy the

moment and not try to turn Mr. Inappropriate into Mr. Right might find that the right man will be drawn to her naturally.

SEX.

The big question: Is it okay to share the cookie with Mr. Right Now? You know in your heart of hearts that he will never be Mr. Right. For many women, trying to maintain a casual mind-set becomes difficult once sex enters the room. The secret to shifting from pouring yourself wholeheartedly into every new relationship is to buy a sex toy, which some of you women will call a back massage, wink wink! It's easy to enjoy uncommitted dating now that you can take care of business at home!

GUILT-FREE DATING.

Some women don't want to worry about getting married right away, but instead are determined to take more pleasure in dating. Mr. Right Now offers lively dating and just plain fun.

This is where women can share their experience of dating Mr. Right Now.

Advice for women who are interested in meeting a Mr. Right Now: If you're motivated to meet him, volunteer at any and every event where you think there'll be a bunch of men—firemen, doctors, entrepreneurs, you name it. You'll do pretty well.

Be careful, most people have baggage. Just don't find the man who has ten Louis Vuitton trunks.

But the truth of the matter is that if you ever want to get past Mr. Right Now and get to Mr. Right, you have to know the secret. It seems like men are all the same, but what really makes the difference is when you find one you can love, trust, and understand. And he returns the favor.

BEING SINGLE.

Being single means different things to each of us. For some, it is a way of life. For a small minority, it is the way we always will be. For most of us, it is a constant battle with optimism. Hope springs eternal, they say. We weren't designed to spend our lives alone. There are some who have dedicated their entire life, for whatever the cause may be, without the desire to marry. And there are those of us who hope that our singleness is temporary.

Being single is not easy. It means first of all that we are daily responsible for every decision we make. We can't share decision making because there is no one close enough to share things with. We trust our friends, but we will not have formed as close a bond as we do in a long-term personal relationship. Therefore, it is up to us to decide what we do each day, whether we go to work, what we will have for dinner, and where we will go for the weekend. We will question what we do on vacation and where and how we socialize.

When we get home in the evening, there isn't anyone there (which is why so often we have cats and dogs) to welcome us. We prepare dinner alone (or don't bother), run a bath or take a shower, and generally live a solitary existence punctuated by our social life and friends as well as work routine. One of the primary issues about being single is not being able to discuss things on our mind when we want to. In social circles we can to an extent, and we may call up friends on the phone, but this lacks the deeper understanding and compassion we receive from a close partner in a relationship.

We like to run ideas by each other, discuss, talk, think aloud, and have pillow talk about the future. All of this is missing when single. Occasional dates or romantic encounters may provide passing closeness, but in effect we remain single still. There is something interesting on TV, but we won't chat about that until we are at work. We have an ailment that worries us, whom do we discuss that with? There is an issue with a person at work, what should we do? Friends and family play their part, but they don't fill that singleness we are likely to feel.

Cooking for one is a painful experience. What is the point of cooking a nice meal if there is no one to share it with? There is a great movie, but we will watch it alone. We need to go shopping and get something new for the apartment, but we are going to have to do without the fun of deciding together. Then of course there is sex. Sex for one is well-known to most singles, but it's generally not what we were designed for.

Close relationships offer companionship, understanding, empathy, and friendship, as well as love and romance; without them, we are pretty much left to our own devices to fill that void. When we are younger, there is so much to focus on that it may not be such an issue, but as we get older we begin to discover that visiting the wonders of the world alone is deeply unsatisfying.

Being single is a heightened sense because our society emphasizes couples. From meals for two in the grocery store to paying for single supplements in hotels, much is set against the single person. Why do we pay extra for a single bed when on vacation? Dinner parties mean we are excluded due to not having a partner, or we are matched up with some geek we have little in common with by friends desperate to pair us off.

Adult society in the West is made up of approximately 33 percent single people, and this is increasing at a remarkable rate. Admittedly, in many areas of the service industry, singles are being seen as a new market, and opportunities to cash in on single life are steadily coming into the marketplace. But again it emphasizes a state of play we may not wish to be reminded of. When single people go outside on the weekend, they see many couples along the way, and this could possibly leave them wondering, "When will I find someone special?" They don't know that for them to find someone special, they have to think that they are special to themselves. And the vibe will automatically send off love signals through the airways.

Therefore, being single means being optimistic, it means keeping positive in the face of adversity. Adversity manifests itself through the thoughts in the back of our head that whisper, "What if?" What if I meet someone tomorrow, what will I do? What if I spend my life alone and never meet anyone again? What if I never fall in love? What if no one actually likes me? What if I were meant to remain single? And it is this whispering that many women fight to keep at bay daily by fighting to remain optimistic.

Optimism comes from the general knowledge that most of us will meet someone. We will find Mr. or Miss Right soon enough. But as we get older, we start to worry, even start silently to panic. If we are to meet our perfect match, it has to happen before we are too old, so we think. We would like it to happen while we are still young enough. When we get closer to forty, it seems like time starts to speed up. In our twenties, time seemed endless. But as the wrinkles at the corners of our eyes demonstrate, one day we wake up and we are older, much older. And we are still single.

Being single is to an extent a triumph; it means we have avoided the disappointment of dating disasters, wrong choices, and loneliness within a terrible relationship. It means we still have our own choices and our own sense of direction. We have the full sense of self-determination and control over destiny. But at the same time it wears us down. It may be hard to admit, but the vast majority of us don't like being single. In fact, we hate it.

We hate it because we don't get to share. We don't get to make happen the sharp image in our head of the perfect relationship we know is possible with the right partner. We have a never-ending well of giving that so far has been ignored. We want to give and we want to please. We wish to love and we want that opportunity. We are ready and willing, but we are not allowed. It's almost like being in an isolation cell in prison. Being single heightens our sense of the need to give and it heightens the sense of frustration accordingly.

Being single isn't a cornfield full of casual sex, boozy nights, general lack of responsibility, and carefree existence over the age of twenty-five. It's a burden that many of us carry. Through failed relationships we have built up a mental list of the things we will never accept again in a relationship, and at the same time it provokes an overpowering explanation of what we really do hope for. Being single isn't about choices; it is about circumstances, and you will find yourself saying, "Oh, Lord, let me see what this fool is all about." We know that had we been in a certain place, had a certain life, then we probably wouldn't be single. But where we find ourselves today means that we are. Well, we are for the time being.

By dating we keep our hopes alive. We realize that there is a light at the end of the tunnel. And while that last man you gave a chance to turned out not to be the one for you, at least you are heading in the right direction. And that's how many of us cope with being single. We do everything we can to keep our hopes alive. We convince ourselves that being single is our choice and we are just waiting to meet the right one. And that's true, that's exactly what we are doing. But the "What if?" whispers away. Our body clock may tick louder, our hair may thin, but we *know* we will get there in the end. We hope.

Being single means living with a sense of frustration that little else can match. We don't have the answers to why we are alone. We even ask "Why me?" This isn't how we envisioned our lives;

this isn't how we saw our future. So why has it happened? What went wrong? Where did we go wrong? Where are all the nice guys and girls? But we still fail to realize that God has a special person for us. We keep judging everyone on the same scale. We need to meet only the right one; we are just going at it the wrong way. So you might as well slip on a comfortable pair of shoes, 'cause the way it is going, this walk is going to take longer than you thought. A word from the wise: If you keep your toenails cut back, the walk will be less painful. It is funny how you can search a lifetime, but God can bring him to you in a day. They haven't all been snatched up. I think the only thing that has been snatched up is your patience and your way of thinking. Then we remind ourselves of the few examples of great friends in great relationships and this provides us with the temporary proof we need. And then we begin to question ourselves further. We may even question our own judgment, wonder if we have missed our best opportunity to be in a good relationship. Maybe we are simply too choosy. Maybe it really is our entire fault. But of course it isn't.

When vacations and national holidays come along, we are reminded heavily just what being single feels like. On Valentine's Day we are also reminded that we are yet again alone this year. However, this year will be different. We feel it. We have our sights set on one or two potentials, and who knows where things may lead? Who knows, by Christmas we could be engaged.

Married people often think the grass is greener on the other side. People in bad relationships dream of the freedom of being single. The only thing that makes me mad is when people say, "I don't know how lucky I am to have my wife." But they don't know that, "My wife is lucky to have me." Sometimes, I want to stop paying these bills to show her just how lucky she really is. But she would try to pay me back and not read my mail or not take care of my business. Well, now that I think of it, "Maybe, I am kind of lucky."

THE SEARCH FOR MR. RIGHT.

Does Mr. Right exist? Is he out there somewhere? Will I find him? It makes you think you are looking for Bin Laden. Mr. Right is a key subject for many women and an inspiration of hope on a daily basis. Yes, he may well exist, yes he is probably out there, and yes you WILL find him! Of course in all our lives we have goals, aims, ambitions, and desires small and large. It is these landmarks and goalposts that keep us positive and busy. It is what makes us human. In recent years, the terms Mr. Right and Miss Right have become overused and devalued. It's almost as if we have a chart on our wall, an extensive tick list, and a résumé of specifics that the person in question must submit to in order to get his foot through the door of the "potentials" interview.

Most of us would deny we are that bad and hope that chance will take a hand in bringing Mr. Right to us. Yes, we accept that we have a small but insignificant "list," and yes, we accept that there are some "candidates" on it, which are nonnegotiable, but they are fairly minor. Or are they? The fact of the matter is that as the decades have passed by, we have become far more sophisticated, as humans, as individuals, as lovers, and as mates. We know how to orgasm, we have a good salary and a nice home, and we are well educated in the ways of the world. Therefore, it is only fair that we seek someone to match, to fit in, to adapt, to accompany, and to facilitate. And there lies the issue.

The fact is that Mr. Right also has a tick list, an agenda, only a small one, of course, but a list all the same, and he is ticking off your assets as we speak. He wants someone young, someone well educated, someone good-looking and in shape. Women are known to be picky and proud, and half of you don't know what you want in a man. My grandmother use to say, "You are going to pick, pick, pick, until you pick s—!" Look at your list and look very carefully at what or who constitutes your Mr. Right. And then look again. Are you sure first of all that your tick list is achievable? Yes, or are you willing to negotiate? Okay, so you are happy with your list. Then what?

Well now, are you willing to go out and get your Mr. Right, or are you waiting for him to come to you? Many women tell me they are waiting for Mr. Right. The word "waiting" concerns me. By waiting, it means men come to you by chance, perhaps by design, and you tick off their assets, you check them out and then cast off anyone who doesn't match your list. Maybe you do, but remember this, my friends: Mr. Right is looking for his Miss Right. How much work have you put into being Miss Right, or should he accept you as you are and fit in around you? Maybe you have Mr. Right, but you don't know how to appreciate him.

As a potential Miss Right, you owe it to yourself to complete a few tasks. Take a long, hard look at your list and ask yourself exactly how flexible you are being. Second, look at who your Mr. Right is and how truthfully obtainable he is. Third, don't kid yourself about your own potentials, but don't compromise on ideals, either. Fourth, bring yourself out into the open, so Mr. Right can find what he is looking for.

Don't play the waiting game, because you do not want to spend the rest of your life knowing your Mr. Perfect is married to someone else when he could have been yours. And finally, compromise is the key in reality. For all the things Mr. Right must be, try and balance that with attempting to be something your Mr. Right doesn't want to miss.

WAIT BEFORE YOU JUMP
INTO A RELATIONSHIP WITH ANY MAN.

When you meet a man and the first thing that comes out of his mouth is, "I'm married, but I'm going through something," or he says, "We're legally separated," right there, hold up and wait a minute, because that is a sign a man is still trying to figure out which way he is going to go. He hasn't made a decision yet. If you get your life all tied up in him and let this man go into your credit cards and drive your car, and he goes back to his wife, you will be left mad, hurt, and maybe even pregnant. You won't quit messing with him if he goes back to his wife, because you are going to feel like she took him from you. Even if he leaves for good, you will wait for him to come back. Save yourself some heartache and don't even get involved with that mess. Get out of the way and let him work it out with his wife. Just tell him that when he gets his life straightened out to holler at you. Remember that oil and water don't mix. Choose one or the other, take the one you like better and get rid of the other. Some people like pain and some people like joy, but you shouldn't have them both.

FROM ONE EXTREME TO ANOTHER.

If you have an addictive personality or behavior, you go from one extreme to the other. It's like eating cakes and pies until you become a diabetic and you are forced to stop. It's like going from one relationship to another, and when you end up with AIDs, then you are forced to stop. You won't have an option, and the decision won't be yours. I am here to tell you today that there is one thing you can do that you have an option on, and that is to run to God. Next time that you decide that you want to be addicted to something, try being addicted to Him. This is one addiction that you won't have to stop.

You can take all you want, and want all you take! Not only can you be addicted to Him, you can overdose on Him. And the good thing about it is that no one can charge you with a crime. Why in the world are you out here looking for Hell, when Heaven is right there staring you in the face? Like the old saying: If it was a snake, it would have bit you. I think the reason it's so easy to go to Hell is that it is for the ones who give up and make excuses to stay down. And I believe it is harder to get to Heaven, because Heaven is expecting something out of you, and you are going to have to change and rise to the occasion.

I used confidence to get me everywhere I have been, and it has guided me in everything I have done. I told people that I was a pimp and ended up a pimp; I told people that I was a bodyguard and ended up a bodyguard; I told people that I was an author and ended up an author. Now I am telling people that I am a speaker, and now I have spoken. So be careful what you let come out of your mouth. Believe me, it can easily happen. But the most important thing that I have found out about this situation is that you have to believe it long before someone else does. Because that is what makes them believe that it is really you, and that's what you really do. You have to eat like that's what you do, sleep like that's what you do, talk and pray like that's what you do, and it won't be long before someone will ask you to do it for him.

When I first told a certain entertainer that I was a bodyguard, I wasn't one, but I dressed the part, and looking at me, he knew that I was big enough to be one. Evidently, it worked, because I was hired as a bodyguard the following week. There was only one problem: I didn't know what bodyguards do. That left me viewing hours and hours of videotapes. When I reviewed those tapes, none of them were the same; everybody did it differently. God doesn't approve of cloning; I'll do it my way. One thing that helped me is that this person hadn't had a bodyguard before, so he didn't know what I needed to do, either. This was a new beginning for both of us. And the moral of this story is: Never be afraid to face anything. Because if God gave it to you, He'll surely make a way for you!

If you are the type of person who never learned to love yourself, and you find someone to love, you will automatically take on his traits, because you don't know what to do. If his love is wrong, then you have betrayed yourself in a loving way. In the beginning I meant for this statement to be for young ladies, but now that I think about it, and what I have seen in the past, so many grown women have not learned to love themselves. They have the same problems that a young lady does. Where are the teachers? The only difference is, they have been living this way for a long period of time. It is bad enough that the world tries to make a fool out of you, but when you join it, you are just twice the fool. And the only way to have a different outlook is to look out. It's like playing dodgeball; you can't be the one who gets hit, because that is when you get taken out of the game.

Ten Fatal Mistakes That Women Make with Their Men.

1.   Having sex too early
2.   Misunderstandings
3.   Overtalking
4.   Making the first call
5.   Introducing him to your loved ones too soon
6.   Telling your kids that he's their uncle
7.   Not asking enough questions
8.   Falling for material things
9.   Letting him know where you live too soon

10. Taking the relationship further when you know you
    don't want him

Let me explain each one of these ten things. I may have covered some of this in other chapters, so please listen because I really want you to understand that you may endanger yourself and put yourself in harm's way if you continue to do these things.

Having Sex Too Early

By having sex too early, you use the leverage and the understanding that you have to make him appreciate you better and to be genuinely concerned about you. And if you have already done it, you'd better hope that he likes you enough to stick around and find out more about you. To most men, you've already given the best part, because that is all they came for. Just remember, the beginning of love always starts off as a game. And when someone gets caught playing, that's when love comes to the end for most relationships, especially if it is in the beginning.

Misunderstandings

It's when you think he loves you, and he loves you not. And all he wants to do is make love to you. That is a difficult misunderstanding. When you want to go to the park and hold hands, his mind is still on going to bed. When you want to go on the shopping spree that he has promised you, he's buying time until he can get everything he wants out of you. You are wondering when he is going to fulfill his promise. Because he already knows that he didn't come to stay, and you will soon find out that you were just in the way.

Overtalking

Why would you tell him everything about you, when you know nothing about him? You might as well give him the strings to your heart so that he can fly you like a kite. Because that is some valuable information that you are giving him, and you don't know the damage you are doing to yourself. I understand that you think he is a nice guy, but what has he done to make you think that? Usually, he hasn't done anything but speak "sweet nothings" to you. It is easier to give him the key to your heart. And giving a man the key to your heart too soon is like giving a thief a key to your home. When it comes to men, it is better to listen and learn than to speak and teach. It's like the old saying goes: If you find a fool, bump his head.

Making the First Call

Once you make the first call, you show interest and make him change his approach to pursuing you, because it is easier now. The phone call has told him that already. He could have been lining up a date to wine and dine you, but now he knows he doesn't have to spend a dime. He's thinking how easy it is going to be to fool you. That date he had planned is over, and he has saved a little money. The date has been reduced to a drink at the coffeehouse. What else will he be able to get out of you? They say that one bad apple can spoil the whole bunch. I guess a phone call can too!

Introducing Him to Your Loved Ones Too Soon

Once you introduce him to your family members, they might adore him more than you do. And they will always encourage you to keep him, because he is putting on a show and seems like the nicest guy in the world. Don't fall for that trick, unless the dog likes him too. Then maybe you could be wrong; maybe your judgment is off. Whether you want to believe this or not, there are still some good men living! And you can still hope that one will walk into your life. It can happen!

Telling Your Kids That He's Their Uncle

You take a guy you like home, and you want him to come in and out of your home, so you tell the kids he is their uncle. But you have taken things to another level. Now, every time they see him, he's coming out of the bedroom and they notice that he is trying to tell them what to do. You decide to reveal the situation after months of enjoyable screaming coming from the bedroom. Now you want them to call him daddy, which leads to a sticky situation and months of conflict. Which will leave your kids saying, "You are not my daddy."

Not Asking Enough Questions

After you have found out all that he wanted you to know, get out the shovel and dig deep for the things that he doesn't want you to know. And when you ask him questions, always look him in the eye, because the eyes are the windows of a person's soul. After the relationship starts, he will never tell. I beg you to collect as much information as you possibly can. Why didn't his last relationship work out? What happened to dissolve it? Get answers!

Falling for Material Things

All of us, at one time or another, have borrowed someone else's car. And when you met him, that could have been his day to borrow the car. And I don't have to remind you that even if it is his car, he might still have car payments, and we all know how that can turn out. He can easily plan to borrow yours six months from now. I have let friends go as far as bringing girls to my house and saying they live there, just to look like they have it going on. When they found out he was lying, I always ended up with the girl, but that's another story. Treat every day like it is April Fool's Day, until you find out the truth.

Letting Him Know Where You Live Too Soon

When you let a man come by your house too soon, and you discover you don't want to see him anymore, it is not as easy as you think to get rid of him, because he has too much information. You shouldn't have to worry that he's sitting down the street or in front of your home when you get home, and end up having to get a restraining order, and you know it takes the police two hours to get there. That system has failed too many women before. So why take that chance, when you can go home and have a good night's sleep? Always give him your cell phone first, so that when he calls you, you can always be on the run. Because if you give him your phone number, he can track you down, and he'll know exactly where to find you.

Taking the Relationship Further When You Know You Don't Want Him

Even if he feels like he's in love, they say that true love never dies, but you can. And if dating isn't fun, the marriage surely won't be. If you know that you don't like him, tell him up front that you just want to be friends. Let him know that you are only looking for a person to go out to eat with every now and then, and maybe even to a movie. Go Dutch; don't ask him to pay all the time. Because if you are friends, friends don't have to take care of you. That's your man's job. Playing with a man's money is like a man playing with your heart. You know how that feels. It can end your life sooner than you think.

WORK ON ONE MAN AT A TIME
AND MAYBE YOU CAN GET IT RIGHT.

My dad used to say to me, "You always got time to do it again but never time to do it right." That made me think. Why do you women always have time to start another relationship because the last one didn't last but a month, this other guy lasted three months, now you have one that lasts four months, and another one that lasts six months? Realize that you have wasted a year and a half or more. Why not just work on one guy for a year and then maybe you can get it right? Don't have sex with him; just enjoy having fun. Go to the park, movies, dinner, and just enjoy talking on the phone. You know, help each other work out problems. Ask a lot of questions and maybe in a year, or nine months later, you might end up with a relationship that means something. You'll never be able to stay in one if you always claim he isn't this or he isn't that, and you always complain about what you don't have and what you need. You are not giving it enough time to find out. Sometimes, if you keep a person long enough, the little things that get on your nerves might turn into the things that you like the most about the guy.

WHEN A WOMAN IS DESPERATE,
ANY MAN LOOKS GOOD.

One thing that bothers me is when a woman loses her patience with God and ends up a patient in the hospital because she picked up the wrong guy. You have to get to know the person you are with. Ask a lot of questions up front. If you were selling your car to a stranger, would you give him your car and trust him to pay you later? All I'm asking you to do is ask questions before you give over your life. You have to learn to listen to what a person is saying from the inside of his heart instead of from the top of his head. If his thoughts are coming from the top of his head and he's talking from the side of his mouth, you will be fooled by him.

DIG DEEP INTO HIS HISTORY.

After he has answered your questions, remember he is telling you only what he wants you to know. This is where you get out the shovel and dig deep for those things that he doesn't want you to know. And remember, when you talk to him, look deep into his eyes, because the eyes are the windows of a person's soul. He won't tell you things he doesn't want you to know after the relationship gets started.

HIS HISTORY WILL HELP YOU
FIND OUT WHO HE IS.

The reason that I think it's important to find out about people's childhood is that it can help explain why they have a lot of outbursts, rage, and anger. For example, when the mother and father divorced, the daddy told the son, "Your momma isn't anything. She does not care about you. I am the only one who loves you." Then the son went and stayed with his momma for a couple of weeks, and she said, "Your daddy isn't anything. I wish I had never married him." This could make a child confused. Or maybe he saw his daddy with another woman while still married to the momma. Or maybe your mate heard his momma's girlfriends poisoning her mind about men. Maybe your mate's new stepdaddy tried to rape him when he was young and now he is traumatized because his momma didn't believe him. Maybe he was beat up by bullies and laughed at by other children and called fat or ugly. There are things we don't know about that happened to a person in his younger days that really affect him in later years.

DON'T LET THE LOOK OF LOVE CONFUSE YOU.

The look of love is on your face. You see it looks good, and love can be good, but what you do not consider along with love are the problems you're going to have along the way. That's why it's so important that you pick somebody who is God-fearing. I know that you want him to look good, but a good personality and kind and considerate ways are just as important. These are the things that you are going to have to depend on when the feelings of love seem to come and go. Believe me, you are going to need more than just looks to keep your relationship strong through the rough parts. Make sure you ask him, "Do you believe in God?" and "What talents do you have?" If he likes to build stuff, that is a good thing. You need that kind of talent in your life because things are going to break. If he has a lot of money and can buy new things or get someone else to fix them, that's a good thing too. All I'm saying is get someone who can fix things or someone who can buy things, 'cause the in-between just don't work. Don't look just at the fact that he's handsome or has a nice body. Looks go away and muscles fall. And then when something breaks, he looks crazy because he can't pay for it nor can he fix it. That's the type of man who will ask you, "What are we going to do?"

TESTING YOUR MAN MAY PROVE
TO BE BENEFICIAL.

I don't know how many times I can stress or remind you that any man can be suave. You have to put some heat on these guys before you get involved with them or have sex with them. Before you marry these men, you have to apply heat. You have to make them a little uncomfortable. Then you will see the true man. Just make him a little uncomfortable, and you will see what he will do in a crisis or how he will do in a moment of anger. This will let you know whether he is really a man worth being with.

ACTIONS SPEAK LOUDER THAN WORDS.

You have to do something to make this man jump into a situation. A crisis is going to happen sooner or later in your life, so why wait until it happens when you can find out what you're really getting yourself into now? Here's a way to test your man. Let the air out of one of your tires at work. Call him and tell him you have a flat. Let's just see what he will do, because a real man will always come to the rescue. He could even bring you his car and say, "Baby, take my car and I'll deal with this." The reason I'm telling you to do it at work is that he'll have eight hours to figure out what he is going to do. But make sure you have a can of Fix-A-Flat because you might find out he doesn't really care.

IF HE MAKES YOU A PROMISE, WRITE DOWN THE DATE.

When a man promises you something, write down the date he said it and then write down the date he changed it. That will pretty much be a record of how many lies you will really have to listen to. If you write down a promise on April 7 and he reneged on it by April 29, you should start to worry that you are not winning this game. Promises are broken often, but part of being a man is keeping your word. Manhood means saying what you do, and doing what you say.

LADIES, WATCH WHAT YOU SAY.

I gather that you get mad enough sometimes to think it's all over, but until you know it's over, watch what you say. Use that "I'm leaving" like it's a gun. They say never pull a gun out if you don't mean to use it. Well, never say you are leaving if you are not going. And if a man says he's leaving, stop acting like you don't care if you do. When he's gone, you'll just start crying. Remember, the more you cry, the less you have to pee. Say what you mean, and mean what you say.

When the man gets another woman, now you run over there like some little wet puppy crying and calling the woman out of her name. It doesn't look good when you start cursing and backing up and begging for a man to come back. Now you are letting him know that he can do you any kind of way he wants to. He's going to lose a lot of respect for you. It would be better if you just stayed gone and let him come back to you on his own. Make sure you don't want him back before you let him go or he leaves. The object of the game called life is it is better to be wanted than wanting.

STOP HOLLERING ABOUT
WHAT YOUR MAN IS NOT.

We say words to each other that should be against the law. I think it's because of freedom of speech. If we started thinking about others' feelings and measured our words, it would have a huge impact on the world. Sometimes men turn to other ladies because the things they do for you may be all the things another lady wants. You can tell me all day what I am not, but why not start telling me what I am? This could be a good man once you let him go. And, after you let him go, you could end up with a suckah.

TALKING AND LISTENING ARE
BOTH IMPORTANT.

A good man will be there for you, but men don't want your everyday problems. Can you spread them out a little bit? I mean, can you just save them up and start out with, "Baby, I want to talk to you about something when you get time," and then just tell him about it in a couple of days. He doesn't want to hear about problems every day. Men don't like it when women act like every day is a 911 emergency call. This could really mess up a relationship 'cause now the man just feels like a filter, like he's just here to solve your problems. What about when he has problems? If your problems take up all of the time, when do you have time to help him with his problems? If you don't ever let a man tell you about his problems, and you are too busy telling him about yours, he could end up telling them to another woman. A relationship has to be give and take.

TEAMWORK.

Let's talk about teamwork, since you think love is a game. The only way you can win a game is if everyone on the team does his or her part. But if someone on the team gets hurt, you have to rework your plan to cover the injured player. At this point in time you have to quit being selfish and go beyond the call of duty. It is the same when you are dating. If your loved one gets sick and can't pull his load, you have to be twice the person until he can get back on his feet. That might mean you have to do some juggling, like taking the kids to school or rushing home from work to take them to their activities, and rushing to the grocery story, or even helping to prepare dinner at someone else's home. And then running back to pick the kids up to come home to eat dinner, while you call your loved one five or six times a day to make sure that he doesn't need anything. I know you are saying, "That's too much, it's not worth all of that."

You have just answered a million-dollar question. You are not ready for love, 'cause love is not selfish, but complaining people are. Ohhh, don't let you get sick; you are in there holding your stomach and asking someone to call 911. You are begging someone to lie beside you, and if he doesn't, you swear to God that he doesn't care about you anymore. Whatever happened to, "You have to give to receive"? Maybe you don't know that rule, because all you have done is receive. So put your feet in someone else's shoes; it might change the way you think and maybe even the way you walk.

I notice that our lives are a lot like traffic signs. Green is for go, yellow is for caution, and red is for stop. The way we live, we are faced with the same warnings. There's nothing wrong with it; it's called instructions. The problem comes in when someone decides to run the red light. If you run the red light, green has no value anymore, because now you just go when you get ready. It doesn't matter what time it is. Isn't that what some men do? You have a great dating relationship until he runs the light. Now he comes and goes as he pleases. Maybe you can play like you are a traffic cop and write him a warning ticket. If it happens again, you know that you can't physically lock him up and put him in jail, but you can surely lock him out of your life and out of your home forever.

IS HE TIRED OF YOU BEING TIRED?

The words that can really damage your relationship are, "I'm tired." You expect someone to understand when you are tired, but you don't understand that he is tired of you for being tired. Who wants someone who is always mentally and physically tired? Then you get mad when he looks at someone with energy. Then all of a sudden you get energy and want to FIGHT. If you had used that energy to laugh and walk around, it wouldn't have to be a fight.

MEN CAN GET SICK AND TIRED TOO.

A lot of time men leave home because they can't take it anymore. It is too much pressure. A person can take only so much, and then it feels like he doesn't even care anymore. He has an attitude that whatever happens, just happens. He will go as far as to say, "Kill me. It doesn't make any difference." That is when you are tired of being sick and tired. It is kind of like pushing a person on a swing. You swing a little harder and harder every time the swing comes back to you. You push a little higher and higher, and one of those times when it comes back, the person is no longer in the swing because he or she has fallen out of it. This is the way you act when you are married or in a relationship and you have gotten tired of it. When you are up high in the air, you decide that it is time for you to get out. You jump off that swing on the ground, and you start walking. The person is waiting for you to swing back, so that he can push you again. But you are no longer there. You have to know when it is time to make a change. You have to know when you have had enough. You have to know that you can no longer deal with this situation. Just stop and face the facts. How is this relationship affecting your life? Is it messing with your health? Is it worth it to keep on pushing until things get better? You are the one who has to decide this.

NO GOOD MAN WANTS TO BE AROUND
A BAD WOMAN.

Your man is to be there for you, but fair is fair. Sometimes you have to quit whining and complaining that "I wish I had a good man." The reason you don't have a man could be the way you are acting. What good man wants to be around a bad woman? Oh, they will stay for sex. As pretty as you are, you are starting fights, and all you want to do is go jump on somebody and get your face all scratched up, cut up, and get all those bruises on you. Something is definitely wrong. There is nothing worse than a man's wife in jail, and how does that look, him bailing his wife out of jail? That doesn't even sound right. It doesn't sound right for your man to be in jail, either, but sometimes a man has to do things to protect his family. You should stop trying to be the leader and the person who tries to protect everything. If you don't let your man be the leader, protector, and man, another woman will.

Friends Can Make Good Spouses.

People always say to marry someone who is foremost a friend. The problem these days is most people don't know what a true friend is. And when you meet someone, you tell others, "This is a friend of mine." Friendship goes a lot deeper than people think. And if you are going to marry somebody because of friendship, you sure better hope you know what friendship is all about. All you have to do is watch his movements. Watch how he treats you and others and watch and see if he is there for you, and that will determine what kind of friend he is.

Give Him a Fair Chance.

Ladies, you are so afraid and worried about what a man has done to you in the past that you won't give the future a chance. There may be a man in front of you right now who is tired of going through changes with women who don't have their priorities straight, and he is searching for something new. You may be that something new, so watch out! He really wants to be that man for someone, and you are afraid to step up to your new position. You have got to let go of the past. My suggestion is that if you are going to give someone a chance, start off new and let the romancing begin.

Know that when things are going sour, you need to stop and check things out to see what is going on. Sometimes, we don't know what is going on, but both people are responsible for the relationship going bad, and both have to find answers and ways to bring the relationship back to the loving relationship it once was, or one that you were working toward. You have to give someone a chance, because if you don't, you are going to be a lonely person for the rest of your life.

THE TRUE MEANING OF LOVE.

Growing up we learned many things. We learned the importance of touch. And then we learned about words and the true meaning of different words. What about the word "love" and its meaning? What does it mean to you when you hear those sacred words, "I love you"? Whether they are coming from your parents or someone you are deeply in love with, these words can melt your heart like no other words can. How many times did your parents tell you that they loved you while you were growing up? Did you often hear these words? What was it like in your household? Many times while we are growing up and maturing into adulthood, we have a false sense of love, and sometimes we don't know how to love. Who taught you about love? Was it real for him or her, or was it real to you? Then you will go out into the world and try to give to others what you have been taught.

Love should be cherished. Think about the people you love in your life and ask yourself if you are selfish. Can love be selfish? If love is free, and free to express, then why don't we give it freely? Why are there a lot of people walking around with frowns on their faces and acting like they don't care if they live or die? Is love pain? I think not. There are many joys in life that come through the experience of love. You feel like you are on top of the world, or you could jump off the highest mountain and still live. Love is like being high, and when you taste just a little of it, you feel like you can conquer the world. When you tell someone that you love him, please make sure that you do.

Love is also action. When you love someone, you want him to know just how much you really do. Maybe at this point in time you can't buy him a Jaguar, but you can afford a Ford Focus. That is the best you can do right now, but as soon as your money status changes, you'll improve your style of car, because you want that person to know that there is nothing in the world that you won't do for him, especially when it is legal. When you love, you will go out of your way to do things. You will even create things so that they are precious and meaningful. So the next time you say "I love you" to someone, just make sure that you do. Just remember, if you teach someone how to love wrong, then he'll give someone the wrong love.

WHOM ARE YOU BLAMING?

It seems like it is so much easier to blame someone else for your being where you are in life. You might want to blame the teacher for you not learning the material she was trying to teach you, but it was not her fault that you were sleepy in the classroom and didn't want to hold your head up long enough to listen and hear the instructions. It is not the teacher's fault. And when you fail all of the college entrance exams and don't meet the minimum expectation to graduate, you want to blame teachers for that too. Did you ever think about your bad study habits or your staying up late at night? So please control it, because once a man sees you in this state, I guarantee you he will run for safety. The only mistake you are making is putting the blame on someone else rather than yourself.

TOO MUCH COMPLAINING.

I like to tell ladies that complaining sets you back. Because the way a man looks at it, he doesn't want to feel like you made him do something by complaining. He doesn't want you getting all up in his behind about a thing. So why don't you be grateful for what someone or God does for you? If you are appreciative, more than likely a man will do more for you because he will be so happy that you are happy with the little that he did for you. Believe me, those things will get bigger. I know you have heard the legendary song "Be Thankful for What You Got." I don't know where it originated, but it is certainly a good principle to follow.

But some women will complain about the item, and tell their girlfriends he bought only this or that, and will describe the sweater or pants that he bought. Some will complain to their mates, "Do you think this is all I am worth?" Maybe, at the time, that was all he could afford. But whatever it is, do like my grandmother said, "Just take it." If you don't like it, give it to someone else, because he might decide to give you something that you really want someday. When you turn down something like it is not good enough, you might be making a big mistake. Who knows what the future holds? Quit being so greedy and difficult when it is time to give something. Just because you cook and clean every day, you want to make a big deal about that. For those of you who don't work, don't forget your man when he is out working to bring the bacon home. Believe me, I am not belittling you, because cooking and cleaning can be a job, especially depending on the demands of your home and how many mouths you are feeding.

WHERE ARE YOU?

Ladies, if your man seems a little lost, just ask him, "Where are you?" Ask him where he is right now and where he is trying to go. Then you will have to give him a shortcut, so that you can help him to get to where he needs to be. Ladies, when your man is trying to give you a helping hand, just let him do it. He may not do it right, but don't forget that he is trying to help you. My wife likes to keep our house sparkling. I don't know how she does it, because she works all day, but she does. She likes the house to look a certain way. I step in and try to help her so that we both can keep the house like she likes it. Guess what, we are both happy. She wins and I do too!

Women like to wash clothes a certain way, so men, when you are helping around the house, please make sure that you sort the clothes a certain way. If you are washing a white load of clothes, and you have gathered the towels, socks, and shirts together, please take the towels out, because you don't wash the towels with socks and underwear. That is a big no-no! Although you are doing a good thing, this will make your woman very angry, and you don't want your good to be evil spoken of. So once again, let us all try and keep the peace.

Ladies, don't go out and try to be Wonder Woman. Wonder Woman is long gone. She was good in her day, but we are living in a new era now. Things are not like they used to be. If you try that Wonder Woman thing, you may come back a wandering woman and a worried woman because things didn't go right. You have to plan before you go out there and try to be tough. What if you try to be tough and he doesn't care about you being tough? Then you are going to be talking about, "I'm sorry," and that doesn't always work. That won't always let you back in. Sometimes a man will discover that he doesn't want you anyway. Remember you left him, and he got over you. So quit trying to get back in. Some things you have to let go and just count them as a loss. We will lose a few things in life, but we'll gain some too. You have to know when to hold and when to fold, because this thing called life is certainly no joke, and I certainly am not playing with my life. That is why I am trying to help women all over the world to come to grips with theirs.

MARRIAGE, A THREE-RING CIRCUS.

They have all kind of jokes out about being married and how tough it is. Marriage is what you make it. I am not going to tell you that there won't be some rough days. There are going to be some good days too. We must make those good days outweigh those bad days. I heard a joke the other day. God said, "Marriage is a three-ring circus. First, you have the engagement ring, then you have the wedding ring, and last you have the suffer ring." You know something that is funny to me, when a man does something to a woman, she'll talk about what she is going to do, and blow it all out of proportion and make it as big as the Empire State Building. When a woman does something to a man, she makes it as little as a bump in the road. Although she may be wrong about the entire ordeal, she won't admit to it, and she'll make you feel that it is okay for a woman to make a few errors. Oh, but the woman will raise plenty of hell just to convince the man that he is wrong. You-all need to stop some of this mess!

MARRIAGE IS BEAUTIFUL.

The beautiful thing is there are a lot of men out there who wish they had a good woman, someone they can trust and go a whole lifetime with. It's a beautiful thing to have a wife. I look at all the precious things that I've acquired in my life since I have been married. I now have beautiful thoughts instead of evil and mischievous thoughts. I really realize how important this is now. More than combined incomes, the wonderful thing is to have someone to grow old with.

IF HE ASKS YOU TO SIGN A
PRENUPTIAL . . . BEWARE.

If he is going to marry you and he asks you to sign a prenuptial, really what he's telling you is, "I think you are the one, but I am not sure." Just in case you are not, you can't leave with all of his stuff. If I were a woman, I wouldn't go for that, because what you can't do when you get married is think, "This is the one, but don't trust her." That's one of the biggest problems with marriages. You keep thinking that's the one because her pants are tight. Men keep thinking that's the one because her hair is long and she's good in bed and she has cooked a little dinner. But men must believe that she's the one because she's been through everyday life, arguments, raising kids, dealing with personal problems through sickness and health. If you are on point with all that, then why do you have to sign a prenuptial? I wouldn't do it. If I were a woman, I wouldn't fall for the prenuptial just to marry that man.

DON'T TAKE ADVANTAGE.

If the good Lord blessed you to marry a man who's wealthy enough for you not to have to work, please do me a favor. Don't spend all of your time shopping for shoes, clothes, and this or that. Come on now, you know better than that. If you've never had much in your life, don't abuse the position you are in now. It is not all yours. Because that is not what this is for. That's not why God blessed you with that man. He has blessed you to bless other people. God didn't bless you with this money for you to go somewhere and just sit down. You can start a foundation or you can help needy kids or sick people with some of his money. Let the man know that you are there for him. Help him to grow as a person, and don't keep taking from the situation. If you are in it only for the money, remember that what goes around comes around.

LOVE IS A BUSINESS.

I think the reason I've survived life so long without being hurt is that I believe what they say: Love and marriage are work. If I ask my wife to cook, or if she asks me to cook, even if we don't want to, love will make us do it. And because we love each other so much, we will come out of our comfort zones to satisfy each other. If you say it's work, then there's some business involved. I came from womanizer to woman adviser. That's a hell of a turnaround. I've learned that in order for a marriage to work, there has to be an agreement on both sides. When I asked my wife to marry me, she said, "I can't marry you until you ask my dad to have my hand in marriage." I said, "You must be out of your cotton-picking mind. As old as I am, I am going to have to ask your dad?" And then I found myself doing it anyway, although I thought it was kind of silly. She stood up for what she believed in, and I had no choice but to go with it if I wanted her. So ladies, you got to push the man a little further and make him do some extra stuff. If he's serious enough to do the extra stuff to be with you, you know he is for real because he is making an investment. When I asked my grandfather, "How do you stay married for so long?" he replied, "You got to let your wife wear the pants and you just try to get in them every now and then."

THE ULTIMATUM.

If your man gives you an ultimatum and says, "It's either this or that," always take "that," 'cause "this" is not working anyway. A crazy man or an ignorant fool can change. What I don't want you to do is sit your behind around waiting on him to change. You want to let him know you're a good woman and you're behind him 100 percent. You can do that and let him know that it's time to move on forward with your life. He'll realize you're the best thing he has ever had in his life, and once he thinks he has changed, he'll come back to get you. And when he does, you should have rules on what you expect of him. If you take a fool like he is, that's what you are going to get out of him. Just remember, when he comes back for you, you have these advantages. Don't go after him, because he'll know you will take him any way you can.

You Don't Have to Put Up with Mess.

They say that marriage is work, so treat it like a career. If and when the arguing starts, treat it like you are the boss and you are on your job. If you treat it like a career, you'll always be trying to better it. Look here, go and get your business cards and explain to your man that you don't have to put up with his mess. Show him that stack of business cards that you have been hiding at work in your desk drawer. Let him know that if he really wants to be with you, you would suggest that he straighten up, so that you can better the situation. Let him know that there are men who are waiting for his job and his position, and that the business cards you have are just as good as applications. Stamped and hired!

On Change.

I think my marriage is thriving because I got a chance to try a new me with a new person. Honestly, I don't know if I would've made it if I had tried to straighten up for my first marriage, because the person had been taking hell off of me for years. Isn't that something how a woman can take hell from her husband her entire marriage and not try to save her own soul? The only way to have a different outlook is to look out.

IMAGINE A NEW LIFE.

The main thing I want to stress to ladies is don't let your could have been mess up your could be. Quit being scared to drop what you have that is not working anyway and know when to let someone new have a chance. You know what the old guy has done, and he's going to keep doing the same thing he was doing. When you find something new and it seems like it's working and the person cares about you, but then an old lover wants you back, don't mess up what you have for something old that never worked. In this case, the grass really is greener on the other side. Give the new person a fair chance. You can go backward anytime you want to; that's easy. But if you go backward, know that there isn't going to be any chance of change. Your heart, mind, and soul will always be in the past. Don't let your past block your future. Don't block your blessings, because God knows what you need and He will put it in your life if you will accept it. You can't worry about what happened last time with a new relationship, because if you do, the same mistakes will get in your way. Because it hasn't been decided yet which one of you caused the problems in the relationship. I am not judging, because I am on your side.

DON'T PLAY WITH A MAN'S HEART
OR HIS FEELINGS.

Don't keep taking the relationship further when you know you don't want him, no matter how big the bank account looks. If you keep dating him without wanting him, at some point it will prove what you are really made of. I know that some women will say, "So, it doesn't make any difference to me." But the man God has for you could be watching the way you are treating the one you don't want.

DON'T TEAR HIM DOWN.

If you decide that you don't want a relationship with a man, and he's been decent to you, when you break up with him, you've got to patch him up before you put him back on the streets. Let him know that he is special and someone out there will love him, it's just not you. Make sure to tell him that he's a good person and y'all just can't make it. Don't tear him down. There are not enough good men to go around, and if you tear one more down, we're setting ourselves back further and further. I'm begging you women, please when you get finished with a brother, at least pat him on his back. Make him feel good about himself before you send him on his way so he'll still be good for somebody else.

YOU CAN END UP WITH A GOOD MAN.

If you take my advice, you could possibly end up with a good man who had a pat on the back. The longest walk in the world started with one step. Now, you have to do what makes you happy, because if you don't do what makes you happy, by the time you get to the end you start to realize how short life really is and you are going to want to hurt somebody for using up the best part of your life. I've said this once and I'll say it again, and I'll keep saying it until you understand. I am trying to stop women from being doorknobs, where everybody gets a turn. You can let just one person turn the knob and walk into your life and live, at least most of the time, happily ever after.

EIGHT

Cheating

HAS LOVE CHANGED?

I have a question for you: Has love changed from the olden days? Have we lied about it so much that it doesn't mean anything to us? Back in my grandmother's day, they talked about only one love and this was unconditional love. In this day and time, I hear tell of ten or twelve different types of love relationships. In the old days, ladies weren't desperate and loose as some women are today. Back in the day, it would almost be a witch hunt to mess with somebody's husband and get pregnant by him. Stealing someone's man or woman was like stealing a vehicle: You knew when they caught you, you were going to have to give it back and you would pay the penalty. Depending on the judge, heaven knows what that would be.

WATCH FOR THE TELLTALE SIGNS.

A man messing around in his relationship is kind of like him buying an extra car. You could owe $20,000 on your old car, but you are ready for a new one because you think the old one is falling apart. They'll tack on the old bill to the new bill. Now, seven or eight years have passed by, and he still wants another car. He is still upside down on the second car, and he has gotten tired of it. Now he wants a third one. It's just like paying taxes. They'll put interest on it, and all that leads to a lot of stress. Tell you what, my player skills were so cold that I used to get lipstick on my shirt and stop at the store and get a loaf of bread. I know what you are thinking, "What are you going to do, eat your shirt?" You-all don't understand how a player's mind works. The bread has yeast in it and yeast removes lipstick from the shirt. This is an old trick that my grandmother taught me while teaching me how to cook. She didn't know she was training a player. You take light bread and rub it on the spot of lipstick and it removes the lipstick. One time, I didn't wipe all the crumbs off my shirt, and I had to meet my girlfriend for lunch and she was wondering, "Why are all the birds following you around?" I had to go into player mode, so I replied, "They came with me to sing you a song." All she could do was smile and hold her hand on her heart, not knowing she had just been played. A lot of brothers didn't know that. So from now on check for crumbs on your man's shirt, or look outside to see if the birds are following him around.

Here is another suckah trick. I was going out every night, and my wife at the time had asthma and could not stand the smell of smoke. I had to get in the shower as soon as I walked in. This gave me a perfect excuse after leaving another woman's house without her ever being suspicious. I had to show her love the next night, because I was fresh out of passion. Even when I got a divorce, I would tell girls I was married so I didn't have to stay over at their house all night. I could come and go as I pleased and had time to mess with other girls. Women fall in love deeper when they think you are cheating to be with them.

IF HE COMES IN LATE AND IS AT A LOSS FOR WORDS, HE'S PROBABLY CHEATING.

One of the worst feelings in the world for a man is when he oversleeps at a woman's house, drinking all night, having sex all night, and has to take that long drive home knowing his wife is going to be up getting ready for work and he's just getting in. I remember coming home at five o'clock in the morning and I knew my wife woke up at six o'clock to get ready for work. I eased in the front door, took my coat halfway off and one shoe off, and then lay down on the floor in front of the door. She was on her way to work and came around the corner and saw me lying there and began to feel sorry for me. She asked me if I was drunk and told me I needed to get up and go in the bedroom and lie down. "How long have you been here?" she asked. I told her, "I don't know." I couldn't believe she fell for it. Or maybe she didn't, because she didn't want to start an argument.

THE TELEPHONE.

I'm telling you that the telephone is a straight lead into cheating. Anytime you're around your man and he doesn't answer that phone, and he says, "Ahhh, I don't feel like talking to them" or "They are getting on my nerves," ask him who it is. This guy can't even tell you who it is because he never thought about trying to lie. He thought you would never ask him that question. I'm warning you, don't reach to take the phone but just know that it's a sign.

If you reach for that phone, you are going to end up with a broken hand. A man would rather pay the hospital bill and go to jail for abuse than let you hear another woman's voice on the other end of the phone. He'll go as far as throwing the phone out the window of the car. And he will put the car in reverse and run over it. When you ask him, "What is wrong with you? Why are you doing this?" he will lie and say something crazy like his sugar level is off, and he needs something to eat. And once again to keep from arguing with him, you'll take him straight to a fast-food restaurant. And you'll tell your girlfriends later on when he's not around about what he did, not realizing that it's not a laughing matter because you are "the fool in love."

IF HE MAKES DRASTIC CHANGES, HE'S PROBABLY CHEATING ON YOU.

When he's not in the norm and doing things he has never done before, this is a big sign. Like wearing extra cologne, dressing up, ironing his clothes, and putting a crease in his pants even before he goes to work. I don't care if it's a Sears suit; somehow he wants it cleaned and ironed so that he can look neat. What happened to all of those old oily clothes he used to wear? Don't forget all the extra hours he's working. He is never late for work; now he's even going in extra early. You are thinking he's really changing for the better. He has changed so much that now he's actually someone else. But then you realize the paycheck doesn't fit the extra hours. I had a friend who would tell his wife he was going fishing but instead he went to have sex with someone else. And when he got home, his wife asked, "Did you catch anything." He replied, "No. I hope not, anyway." I said that to remind you to believe half of what you hear and all of what you see.

This rule can also apply to your kids. Once they start dating, they will show some of the same signs when they become sexually active. When you find out about your kids having sex, how can you stop it? So why act a fool and start jumping up and down like James Brown? Don't try to hurt them with words; help them with condoms and knowledge.

HOW TO CONFRONT HIM.

Ladies, if you go searching for your man and find him up to no good, I want you to calm down and still be classy women. Today's technology has exactly what you need. Instead of calling him, text message and take your camera and take a picture of his car and location, then go back to the house. When you question him and ask him about his whereabouts, and did he receive your text message, just wait for his answer. If he says he was at a friend's house, pull out your camera phone and show him the picture. Tell him it must have been a girlfriend. You have the pictures to prove it. Don't let him hold your phone at this point, because he'll probably destroy it. Just enjoy the hurt look on his face. I'm sure he didn't expect that from you.

IT'S BEST TO BACK OFF WHEN THE TRUTH STARTS TO HURT.

When you know your man is cheating and you have caught him in a lie, he might get a little angry at you and get up in front of your face, because you are getting closer to the truth. If that starts to happen, just back off, don't push him. The truth hurts, but I don't want you to be the one getting hurt. If you keep pushing him and yelling and screaming, something can happen. As long as he knows you know, you shouldn't feel like a fool. Whether he shows it or not, trust me, he feels like one.

IF YOU'RE FIGHTING ABOUT A MAN, HE'S PROBABLY NOT YOUR MAN.

If you are arguing, fussing, and fighting with some woman about your man, it's not your man. There is no need for my wife to argue with another woman. If you catch my wife arguing with another woman, it must be about her husband because it sure won't be about me. For better or for worse, I am her man. If somebody starts an argument with us, we both are going to address it. We'll end up taking care of it ourselves. Don't anybody call me, because I don't have anyone else.

WHEN SOMEBODY TELLS ME SOMETHING, I WEIGH IT OUT.

If someone comes to me and says my wife is cheating, I weigh it out first. I find out which side of the story weighs the most. So when you say, "I didn't do it," and somebody tells me you did, that's just your word against his or hers. But if four or five more people witnessed it and they tell me what time and where it happened, and who was there and whom it happened with, then now it's a fact. Even the forensic scientist will agree to that! You can get that information okayed in any police department in the country.

YOU'RE THE ONLY ONE WHO KNOWS WHAT YOU CAN LIVE WITH—AND CAN LIVE WITHOUT.

You are the only one who knows how much you love him. You're the only one who knows if you get rid of this man, you can't pay your bills because he's taking care of you and those kids. You are the only one who knows that you don't have anywhere to go because your momma is mad at you for being with that man because she told you that he was not any good. I cannot tell you to leave or stay. But plan carefully. Get yourself a really good plan to leave or, if you are going to stay, decide how you are going to put up with this for the rest of your life. That's the only advice I can give whether you should get rid of your man or not. Half of you are not going to do what I said anyway. Some of you make enough money on your own, but he lives with you and you are still afraid to put him out, which leaves you asking someone, "What should I do?" And when your friend maps out an excellent plan for you, your crazy behind will still say, "I don't think that is going to work, because I need him." You have a slave woman mentality, thinking that a piece of a man is better than no man at all. And I do specify that it is only a piece. And that piece is not as good as you think it is. You just think that trying something new will get you hurt. Like my grandmother once told me, "A hard head will make a soft behind."

SOME WOMEN GO AFTER MARRIED MEN.

Women can make a good man a suckah. Some women are good at this; they have different techniques they have practiced over the years. It starts out real simple. First they ask, "Are you married? Have you ever thought about cheating? Have you ever thought about being a sugar daddy on the side?" Then they go in for the kill. They say, "Let's try it, I'm sure it will be fun," while they are licking their lips and blinking their eyes. It's even worse when they work with you, and you have to see them every day. You end up seeing them more than your wife, because she's out of the house working so you can have the American dream. Every now and then, if a man is not secure enough in his own marriage and with his own self, he is going to slip. It's hard not to slip. You have to be really close with God. The thing is, ladies, once a man hears a woman begging every day, we start thinking, "Maybe I'll mess with her so she can leave me alone and shut her mouth." But then, if my wife found out, I know she'll never shut hers.

A PHONE CALL FROM THE OTHER WOMAN.

When your relationship is going good, everything is fine. All the bills are paid, and you are traveling to the islands, to the movies, dinners, and the kids are happy too. Don't let any other woman call your house with some mess. Don't let her tell you stuff like, "Girl, I just want you to know that me and your man are messing around." Just say to her, "Girl, was it good?" and let her know how lucky she is, because you have him at home with you and you are so happy. Ask her, "Did he take you to Jamaica? Did he take you to Africa? Girl, just wait until he takes you to these places. You are really going to see something special and wonderful. When he takes you, you'll know how much he really loves you." Just go along with it! Don't let her run you out of your house. You don't want her to be having fun with your man while you are sitting over there crying and having some ignorant woman trying to take away your dream so that you can get in the corner and talk about what a good man you used to have and what he used to do. I understand that you are mad while all of this is going on. You can't let her know that she has the power to tear your home up. But when you get home, you can tear up everything in the house until you get your point across. I mean you can stop the chatter and get down to the matter. I'm saying, ladies, never let her see you sweat, but when you get home, make your man sweat like hell.

FOR THE WOMEN WITH MARRIED MEN.

You want him because he belongs to someone else. And, boy, you are headed for one hell of a ride. And he will ride right beside you, because he can have his cake and eat it too. Your holidays will become the loneliest days on earth, because he owes them to his wife. If you convince him to be only with you, it won't be long before the shoe is on the other foot. What I'm saying is, it won't be long before he's cheating on you.

WIVES CHEAT TOO.

I have got to stand up for the brothers too, because they are not the only ones who cheat. Wives have been cheating for a long time. I can't tell you how many wives I messed with. It's just not as talked about as men messing around. And if you want to take this thing a step further, now married couples are doing this thing called "swinging." That is where a couple swaps spouses with another couple, which might seem like a great idea at the time.

SWINGING CAN LEAVE YOU WITH
THE SHORT END OF THE STICK.

This is perfectly fine if you are doing it as a couple and you both agree to this. But when reality sets in, nine times out of ten someone will be left upset. Most men are selfish and will mess with the other woman behind your back. Also, they are used to having you and other women too, so when it comes time to share you, it's a problem. I have seen a lot of homes break and tear up with this kind of carrying on. What if the woman in the other couple looks real good and the man doesn't? Now you have to mess with this sloppy-looking guy while your man is lying up with this beauty queen. That is not going to work out well. This is something you really have to think about. The old saying is true: Two is a couple, three or more is a crowd.

DON'T GET MAD AT THE OTHER WOMAN.

Ladies, instead of getting mad when another woman takes your man, I want you to put it in your head that "if she can beat me rocking, she can have my chair." That will help you if and when your man leaves for another relationship. You can just go on with your business. There is somebody else for you who will want you just as much as you want him, especially if you believe it!

A WOMAN CAN DO WELL BY HERSELF, SO
DON'T LET HIM BACK IN YOUR LIFE TOO SOON.

There's a saying, "I can do bad by myself." Why would you want to, when plenty of women are doing good by themselves? You feel a lot of pain when a relationship ends, but just go out and get yourself some good music and listen and dance to it. Pump yourself up and get to know yourself. You can cry, but don't cry for too long. Tears don't solve any problems. If that man asks you to come back, and you aren't sure whether you can forgive him, make him go the long way around. Have him take you to dinners, church, and counseling. If you let him back in too fast and too easy, he will only repeat what he did for you to leave the first time.

Cheating when you are in a relationship reminds me of a red shiny apple. It looks so nice and so good, and once you take a bite out of it, you can't stop eating it. You may want some more of it, but it is going to turn brown on you. That's what happens once you or your spouse starts cheating. The grass only looks greener on the other side. Once you do cheat, there is a chance you can turn it around some kind of way. A person's trust has been violated, and one of the hardest things to do is forgive another person for breaking your heart. Even if he does forgive you, he won't forget. If you cheated and have found a person who forgave you and didn't bring it up again, you must know that you have found a godly person. God is the only one who can make it happen, because it was almost murder she wrote in my heart.

And Remember, Watch What You Do.

You have to be careful what you do and say. So say what you do, and do what you say. People are always watching and looking. You never know where people are and who sees you, especially if you are doing or saying something that you are not supposed to be saying or doing. Remember, just as God is watching the things we do and say, people are too. God watching us should be enough to keep us straight. With people watching too, you are really getting into a mess. It almost makes you think that you can get into more trouble with people than you can with God. I tell you one thing: The way people judge you is going to be different; I believe God will add a little mercy sometimes. And on top of people judging you, the whole world will know!

NINE

Abusive Relationships

WOMEN SAY THEY WANT A ROUGHNECK.
Women will get those thug brothers, and when they find out they are a little too thuggish for them, and always in trouble, they can't seem to leave them. Talking about, "But I can't, I love him, and he is my soul mate." But if you keep letting him abuse you, hang around long enough, you'll end up being someone's cell mate. Quit searching for a roughneck, before you end up with a broken neck. You know, I just want to do God's work. I have been told that the Bible says, "The harvest truly is great but the laborers are few." And I just want to be one of those laborers. I really do want to help and reach out to women all over the world, to help them change the way they are doing things and bring them to a safe point in their lives. I will be that vessel that the Lord can use any day and anytime.

LIKE A GAME OF GOLF.
A man who abuses women reminds me of the rules of golf. You hit the woman, knock the hell out of her, then go find her and hit her again, until she goes where you tell her to go. That's the same thing they do in golf. They hit that little white ball, then go find it just to hit it again to make it go where they want it to go. I'm not saying anything bad about golf, just don't you be the ball.

FIND A MAN WHO KNOWS
HOW TO USE HIS HANDS.

Every time I go to do something, my hands are so big that I get a cut or scratch on them. I love to work hard lifting, moving, and building things. One might think that I have been in a lot of fights, but that's in the past. But I don't want you to be deceived and think that men with nice hands won't hurt you. Those could be the kind of hands that kill with weapons, or pay someone else to do their dirty work. Those nice ones. Wow!

LOVE AND LICKS DON'T GO TOGETHER.

Ladies, the first thing a man will do after hitting you is say, "I'm sorry. I love you." In your mind, you are saying, "I know you are a sorry, poor excuse for a man, but when are you going to apologize?" But love and licks don't go together. They just don't match. But here's one of the biggest problems: You pretty much know when the hitting is coming, so why do you keep pushing forward? Women will keep pushing that button to make him mad because you are angry. At some point, ladies, you have to shut up and live or let it cool down, so you can live to see another day. Come on, now, having the last word is not really that important.

We all have to work together on this thing. If you know he is a fool and you keep pushing him hard like that, what do you expect him to do, be a man and walk away? It is not right for him to hit you, but it also is not right for you to push the buttons that you are pushing.

TOO MUCH PRESSURE.

These days, there is too much pressure on people. They are already hurting and mad that life is not going right. They are broke, having a hard time supporting their families. Their credit is bad, and they are on the verge of suicide, and then you are there pushing them to the outer limits, or should I say the ultimate limits, and that is death, and it may include you, depending on how far you are pushing them to that outer place. Wow! What you are doing, ladies, is not good. Don't push them!

When you push a man, you must expect him to push back. A lot of women talk about how "you let a man hit me and see what happens to him." I really don't think that you know what you are wishing for. All you are going to do is call someone to come and get him. You really are not going to do a thing. He knows that the popo will be on his back in a heartbeat, and you know that as well. He'll be exactly where you set him up to go, and that is in jail.

Quit Blaming Everything on the Man.

The biggest problem I'm having with this is that you ladies are always hollering that the man abused you. Okay, the physical abuse must be stopped immediately, but the mental abuse will never stop because it is a two-way street. It is hard for a person to argue by himself. If you are cursing me just as well as I'm cursing you, this will be a great time to use your disappearing act. Why is my cursing worse than yours? Okay, let's take domestic violence. I have this thing that we need to stop men from hitting women, and we need to stop women from hitting men too. All the physical and mental abuse needs to stop. But the thing is, it will more than likely go on forever, because both sexes engage in this kind of hostility.

One time, when my wife and I were arguing, she said something that shocked me so bad, I took my right hand and placed it in the center of my chest like a woman. It's mental abuse when I go off on her. But when she goes back off on me, she claims she is only trying to help me understand what I'm doing to her and what's wrong with the way that I would be talking to her with no respect. She would give me the same verbal and mental abuse back, then, when things cool down and we are better and on laughing terms, she would say, "How did you like your medicine?" You women need to stop the double standard and cut this mess out. We all got to work on this. I'm trying to tell you this is a joint venture.

DON'T GIVE HIM THE CHANCE
TO HIT YOU TWICE.

Being in a violent situation is almost like getting hit by a car. Let's look at it this way, would you let the same car hit you three or four times? I mean at some point you are going to get out of the way, right? They say lightning never strikes twice in the same place. Then why are you sitting there waiting on a man to strike you again?

WHAT YOU DON'T KILL WILL KILL YOU.

You have this man in your life beating you, misusing and cheating on you. If you don't kill this relationship, it will kill you. I am not saying to kill the man; kill the relationship. It's interesting that when you get a cut, scratch, or scrape you use medicine and bandages to seal the wound on the outside and try to protect it by using cocoa butter. Even when the scar is on the inside, women think they can take medicine for that too. But the scars that a man has put on your insides have to be prayed out. If you don't stop what you are doing, what you are doing will stop you. If you can't leave right away, then ease away from him day by day. When you finally walk away, let it bring the greatness out of you, so the guy can see that he made a major mistake when he lost you. He'll know he made one when he sees that he lost you and is now sitting in the penitentiary counting the days on the calendar with no one to visit him.

DOMESTIC VIOLENCE.

Let's change the subject a little and talk about domestic violence. Let's talk about you getting caught with another person and your man goes off the deep end and ends up slapping you out of anger. Well, anger is one of those emotions that is hard to keep inside of you, and it has to come out of you. Some people have control of their anger, and oftentimes those who are hurting never control theirs. Anything can happen once anger and hurt meet. When you see that a man is mad enough to hit you, just try to calm him down by admitting your wrongness, tell him how sorry you are, and ask him to forgive you. This is not the time for you to be tough and throw up in his face what he has done in the past. It is a time and place for all things, and this is definitely not one of them. Don't act like you are so bad and tell him to hit you. Please don't tempt him. He just might knock you out. This is certainly the wrong road to go down. And don't push your luck, because at this point, he may not care about the end results, although he might think of them after you're on the ground!

You think you can handle a few licks because you are thinking, "I used to fight all the time." But school licks are different from grown licks and a lick from a man. At this point, you should try to keep the peace, so that you won't have to deal with this anymore. There are many people who have gone on to glory or that other place because they didn't know when to shut their mouths. Please use wisdom when you are dealing with a situation such as domestic violence. Being quiet might save your life.

Your Children

DON'T WAIT UNTIL IT'S TOO LATE.

Don't wait until your daughters get their hearts broken and then you try to run in there and pat them and try to patch it up real quick. Give these girls something to fight with, so at least they know. It makes me angry when I talk to women about sharing this information with their daughters ages fourteen and up. They say, "They don't need to know this information yet." But someone has already told them, so when she lets her foreplay become her first time and ends up pregnant, you have to take her to court to plead her case for child support. But if you had passed on this information, you wouldn't have a case to plead. Don't help raise another generation of dysfunctional people. I'm trying to help mother and daughter, because if you don't know, your daughter won't either, because she is learning from you.

SOME WOMEN DON'T
TAKE CARE OF THEIR CHILDREN.

Some of you women leave your kids all alone. They don't even know you. It's Cheerios everywhere, apple juice all on your doggone new couch. I mean, they are making so much noise that you are in there sleeping with earplugs on. And when you finally try to discipline them, you realize they're crying for their babysitter thinking it's their momma, because you have enjoyed half of their lives running the streets, chasing behind some man, or somewhere trying to impress your boss by putting in sixteen hours a day plus weekends. What about those kids you say you love? Now you are so tired that all they hear now is "Be quiet, I am trying to sleep." It seems like a waste of time, because your finances never changed.

NO ONE KNOWS THE TROUBLE I HAVE SEEN.

Sometimes parents get caught up with disciplining a child so hard that they don't realize that they are damaging the child. Things may have happened so very young in your life that you didn't get the things you needed to mature. And most of our parents have told us something to hold us back in life. You don't know it until you grow up and look back on your life and ask yourself, "Why have I been stuck in the same position for the last ten years?"

My father told me, "You'd better learn how to put a shovel in your hand, because a pencil will never fit." Well, he was right; a pencil never did fit, but the money from the shovel and the broom that he jinxed me with had to bury him. I wish we could understand how important words are and how they can lift you or damage you, depending on what they are. He could read and write and still died broke. The funny thing is, even though I had no education, I always had a business mind and have always done my own thing, even if I had to work and have something on the side. And now I have messed around and written a book. Growth will do that for you, especially if you keep reaching for it.

Parents get so caught up trying to feed and protect their children that we are still not covering all the basics. We are dealing with too much surface stuff, never really penetrating their thoughts or what's in their mind. This day and time, kids are faced with so many things. In elementary school, the kids are faced with low self-esteem and identity problems. I can remember when I was that age that I was so confused that I wanted to die. I took my cap gun into the restroom and pulled my pants down and sat on the toilet.

With the thoughts that were going through my head, I knew it was going to be a mess, and you know what I am talking about. I proceeded to put the gun in my mouth to see what it felt like to commit suicide. I pulled the trigger and shot the gun. I told you it was going to be a mess! The gunpowder burned my lips and tongue so bad; I was too hurt and nervous to wipe myself. So you never know what is going on in the back of a child's mind. Children are trying to find out who they really are. If we don't help them find out who they are, they will try to fit in with anybody. One of the biggest problems can be that some of us parents have already tried to fit in with everyone, and we are still trying to find out who we are. And once again, we are teaching them what we know. No wonder the kids are having problems.

In middle school or junior high, they are faced with sex, drugs, belonging to some group. At this point, they are willing to do anything to fit in. They want to belong to something, and at this age they think they know everything. In their mind, nothing can hurt them. They will take a greater chance trying it all, which makes parents frustrated and angry enough to surrender to this kind of foolishness. But no matter how bad it gets, you can't let go. The only way that you can get inside of them is to win their trust. Make them think that you are on their side. Also share with them a story or two of what you did in the past so that they will think that you are human. Be careful how you say it because it might backfire on you. They might say, "You did it and so can I." Don't spend so much time trying to make them think that you are more than them. Spend more time letting them know at one time you were them. You have to let them know that this phase in their life will pass and you are there to teach and support them.

So now your problems and your kids are getting bigger. High school is a different situation. One of the problems is that kids don't realize that they will be making some major decisions like whether to go off to college or move out of the house completely. Or they will enter the workforce. Some will even join the armed forces. This is a serious situation. At this point, all playing must stop. In high school, you will have kids making grown-up choices. Parents can no longer hold their children's hands and walk them into places. You have to let them go. Most kids don't want their parents around at this point. You will hear, "Mom, can I borrow the car?" I know you hate for that to happen, but at some point you will have to trust them. Every once in a while, though, you will still have to check up on them. You never know when you have raised a big liar. Of course, you'll say they learned it from their dad.

At some point a boy is going to ask your daughter for something you have been asking her to save for marriage. Just hope that you have instilled enough in her to say no until it is the right time. You'll know if she does it. It won't take long to find out, because all hell will break loose. It could even cause a mother and daughter to go at each other's throats. You will hear things like, "You can't tell me what to do," which will tear your heart out, but try to be calm enough not to tear out hers. You know what your mother told you years ago: "One day you will have a daughter, and you are going to reap what you sow."

You have to work on this situation like it is a job and you are doing overtime. They will be out of your house soon, living their own life. The only thing you can do is watch, and some of the things you see will be painful. I guarantee you if ask them, they have seen you do some painful things too. No matter what you each have seen, a daughter still needs a mother's love.

Know that drugs will follow some of them the rest of their lives, whether they are involved with them or not. Someone will always know where you can find them. Almost every family has lost one of their members to drugs or some other kind of foolishess. I have done drugs, and it only seemed like it helped the problem I was having at that time. But after the drugs wore off, I had two problems: the problem I had from the beginning, and a drug problem. Let's hope that you have instilled enough fear, values, and morals so your children don't become statistics.

GET CONTROL OF YOUR KIDS.

It takes a little more being their momma, and less being their friend. You got them spoiled and crying because they can't have something, or because they can't have their way. Now you want a man to come into your life and keep providing everything your children want because that's the way you started them off. I'm not doing it. I'm going to stand up and be a man and say what you can and cannot have or do. That shouldn't break us up, but you will let it because that's your baby. But one day your baby is going to leave home and will be living her own life and doing her own thing, and you won't have a man because you gave your man up, trying to be your baby's friend, instead of being your baby's momma. Remember that most successful women had mothers who raised them with a strong hand.

KIDS CAN MESS UP YOUR LIFE.

When you have bad kids, it can really mess up the life you can have with a good man. 'Cause men have a lot of stuff going on in their lives. We just want a wife and some beautiful kids and to go on vacations and come home. We want the children to say, "Hey, Dad," when we get in. But we don't want to start with the problems. Things are different when the kids belong to both of us. Men don't want to come to your house and your boys are gangbanging and robbing stores or jumping on their momma. The man feels as if he has to address all this stuff. He'll end up doing something to the boy and now his life is turned all around and upside down, because he is in jail for hitting a kid or doing something weak. Kids can mess up a good relationship. It's the same thing for a woman. You don't want to go with a man with bad daughters who are calling you out of your name and disrespecting you. Because you know you are crazy and you already know what is going to happen. Now he's sitting up in jail for trying to love someone.

TEACH YOUR DAUGHTER HOW TO BE A WOMAN.

Pay attention to your daughter because she is learning from you. If you teach your daughter love and respect and how to walk and talk and how to comb her hair, and get her used to doing these things when she becomes a young lady, you will build up her confidence and she will love and respect herself. When she starts combing her own hair every morning, she'll grow up to be a woman with a nice hairstyle. Otherwise, you are going to have a nappy-headed daughter, and she will grow up to be a nappy-headed woman. And I want you to teach your daughter the right way to sit and when she has a dress on make sure she sits with her legs crossed. A person shouldn't be able to tell you the color of her underwear at any point in time. It seems like most girls don't care anymore; they just sit any kind of way in dresses.

If you don't start teaching them early, you'll have a woman sitting in the club with her legs open. If you don't teach her to bathe properly, you'll have a stinking woman sitting somewhere invading someone's space. And all of these things are a suckah's dream. It lets him know that she needs attention because no one ever cared. Make sure that your child understands the value of education and how important it is to go to school and pay attention, even though smart girls do dumb things. Just make sure they understand the importance of trying to do it right the first time.

WOMAN BODIES, LITTLE GIRL MINDS.

Nowadays, little girls can look like grown women and a lot of guys take advantage of that. Instead of saying, "I know she's a kid," they are saying, "Man, look at that right there." I have to admit that while they may be little girls, they don't act like it these days. That's why moms need to get involved in their daughters' lives so that they can teach, lead, and guide the girls down the right path. You see your daughter leave the house with her skirt hiked up in the back and her shirt tied in a knot in the front. I guess it doesn't bother you because you are probably the one who bought it. Just know this: A grown man will probably ask your underage daughter for sex at an early age. You have to keep your daughters from rushing into womanhood. And teach them every step of the way. You should make it a point to teach your daughters something valuable about life every day of yours.

BREAKING THE CYCLE.

There is something that really bothers me and that I'm asking God to help me with because it's eating me up inside. I remember the young ladies I used to mess around with and have run over in my life. Now their daughters are grown and I'm watching them go through the same pattern of getting beat up and running the streets and just not caring about life. I had to pray on it because I started feeling like it was my fault because I was the one who showed it to them by doing their mothers that way.

KIDS AND TECHNOLOGY.

There's a certain amount of information you need to know so you can hand it down to your kids, so make sure someone grown in the house has enough experience with technology to check what today's kids are doing. We need to talk to our kids about the internet and the various websites. Teach them not to put negative things on there like their body parts, or have their sexual preferences disclosed or, God forbid, their gang associations. This way later on when they are out there trying to get a job, these things won't come up on their background check. You might think it's nothing now, but if you know like I do, problems show up when you don't want them to, or when you least expect it.

You should have someone email your child under a fake name and age, and talk about meeting him for sex. You would be surprised at the response you will get. But don't kill your child the first day; let it go as long as you can. Then you'll realize how much danger your child is in. You might learn something about yourself, like you are working too much and are never home. Working too much and never being home leaves children thinking on their own, which could lead to a dangerous situation. They say, "It takes a village to raise a child." But now you have to be scared of the village.

The reason you have to teach them when they are young is that predators seek the young and the old. Let's say your daughter wants to be a model. You don't think that some suckah is trying to talk her into taking naked pictures for the camera, telling her that it goes with the job? What if she wants to be an actress? You don't think some woman or man is trying to get her to lie down on a casting couch? That's how a lot of movie stars were created, by selling their souls on a couch in a person's office with enough power to say yes or no.

GRADUATION.

Graduation is a time that brings family and loved ones together. I recently attended my nephew's graduation; he was graduating from elementary school to middle school. I had a flashback. I don't know if they had that when I was in the fifth grade. Oh, my bad, I'm tripping, it was probably because they had put me back a couple of times. I wasn't in a graduation, I was in a situation. I am pretty sure after trying it two or three times, they just push you on into the next grade. What's the celebration for? If they did have a celebration, everyone who came to see you would be saying, "It's about time."

I am going to tell you something else that is going to trip you out. I didn't have a graduation in high school either. All I could remember was the principal saying, "If you make all F's, you are still graduating this year." It was so funny to see a grown man take my grade card and change the Fs on my report card to As and Bs. I guess I got a little too old dating those younger girls. I guess they were tired of looking at me. After he finished, my grade card was looking good, but they still wouldn't let me walk across the stage with a cap and gown. They treated me like I was a bird that flew in. They took me outside the door and told me to fly away. I knew doggone well not to try college, because that was going to take so long to finish that I would be sixty-five looking for a job, and that would have messed up my retirement money.

BE CAREFUL WHOM YOU LET HELP
RAISE YOUR KIDS.

Ladies, if you have kids, the man in your life is the same man you are choosing to discipline and whup your kids. That's a situation that will surely start a problem in your home. He might not know how hard to whip them and when to holler at them. Your kids may need to be raised for another ten years, eighteen years, or whatever, but you should see how he's going to handle situations with your kids first before you marry him and allow him to discipline them.

BABY MOMMA DRAMA.

When a man has baby momma drama, I don't know if you really should be calling that a weak man. I think you should call it a good man, because if you were to have a baby by him and then break up with him, you know that he just won't dog you out or take everything from you and throw you out of the house. I'm just saying maybe you should show a lot more consideration to a guy who takes mess off his last woman with the kids.

SONS NEED A STRONG FATHER FIGURE.

If your man and your sons were never raised by a good father, or had no father at all, how can they learn to be men? There's no one to sit down and teach them right from wrong. I know you're trying, but you can't do it alone. That is where a lot of momma's boys come from. But where do you find a strong man these days? If you don't have a good man in your life, you have to reach back through the bloodline in your family. There has to be one in the family that you can count on. Although your brother might be on crack and your uncle a child molester, if you search hard enough, you'll still find one standing.

WHAT YOUR SONS WEAR.

I get angry every time I see a young man with saggy pants on. I'm six six and three hundred pounds, and I'm the one who needs those pants. He is wearing them trying to be in style and I get up half naked cause they have bought my size out. Do you know what a big man with tight pants looks like? Next time your son leaves the house sagging, let him know there's a big man somewhere who needs those pants.

TIMES HAVE CHANGED.

Back in the day, there was so much love and respect because we needed one another. We still honored our forefathers' legacy from slavery, money wasn't as plentiful as it is today, which proves further that money rules the world and makes some people act a fool. We went from raising our own gardens to not having time to raise our own kids. You couldn't go down the street and start something, because the whole neighborhood would beat your behind all the way home. The house was always crowded and you couldn't do wrong, because everybody had his or her eyes on you. Nowadays things are a little different.

Grown-ups can't even go on their porch or down the street, to visit the neighbors, because the kids will whip your behind all the way home! I think some of the reasons kids have so many problems in school is that the problems are in the home as well. Once your kids see you fighting and arguing, then they go to school and think that's the way to handle their problems.

DON'T LET YOUR KIDS SEE YOU DO DRUGS.

If you are addicted to drugs, I'm begging you to go into rehab, because your family needs you. Your kids and your parents, if they are still living, need you. Sooner or later drugs will catch up with you, and you will end up dead or in the state penitentiary. You don't want someone else taking care of your kids. You don't want your kids to belong to the state. It sure doesn't teach kids that drugs are bad for you when they see their own mother and daddy do them. There is no excuse for that. It's bad enough that people outside the home will try to introduce drugs to them without you doing them inside of the home.

CARE FOR YOUR KIDS.

I'm tired of women letting men hold their babies while they go hide their purses. What about the child? Is the child important at all? Will you put a man before your child? Would you rather something happened to the child than someone taking your purse? What is more important, the purse or the child? Seems like we have gotten a little confused about a few things in life, and somehow these things have us all twisted up. Another thing about women is that when they get a divorce from a man, and the child looks like the daddy, they begin to hate that child because of whom the child reminds them of. Women say they don't do this. There are so many things women won't admit to, but if that child could reveal some of the things that you say to him or her, they may lock you up somewhere. Please get the help you need after a divorce so that you can help your children remain sane. Don't take it out on the children, because they didn't ask to be here. Don't use them as a bouncing ball. You chose that man and there had to be something that attracted you to him and something you loved about him.

HEAR YOUR KIDS OUT.

We need to change the way we look at our children, because we think that they should be still playing at fifteen years old. But the world doesn't have room for those childhood games anymore. If they are fifteen and still playing, the world will pass them by. Everything is moving so fast that we can barely keep up. You can buy a brand-new computer today, and thirty days later it seems like it's outdated. I think you should let your kids' creativity come out at a young age and try to help them with their struggle. Because if you help them, you never know what they will be when they grow up, because they like what they are doing. So many times we don't agree with what they want to do, and we send them back to playing, often stunting their growth potential and their ideas of becoming someone great or famous. Brilliant kids come from bad situations, but there are so many who don't that I'd like them to have a fair chance too. One thing I think could help them is the environment they are raised in. So many times we spend all we have on the way we look. If you work harder trying to get your kids in a safe environment rather than working on the way you look, in the long run the way your kid advances and feels will still have you looking good in a different way. My daughter is thirteen years old now, and we are encouraging her to shoot an etiquette tape on teaching children how to eat and sit properly. Not only will it help the kids; I'm sure it will help some grown-ups as well. Many of us can use some tips on that subject. We are definitely boosting her confidence, because she may be able to pay for her own college tuition, instead of waiting on me to write her a check for college. There is nothing worse than two people waiting on one check.

ELEVEN

Things I've Noticed:

BOOM'S WORDS OF WISDOM

I know doggone well that I am not a Preacher,
and I am not a Preacher's son,
but I'll do the preaching
until the Preacher comes.

You know, the funny thing is that I've met plenty of people with money who were unhappy and never met God. I've also met plenty of people with no money who were very happy and close to God. Being happy is more important than material things. If you were raised in a low-income environment, all you have to hold on to is your pride. We are proud people because a lot of us are raised poor. You'll still have pride when you accumulate the fame, houses, and cars. We're taught to be cool, calm, and collected in the most difficult situations. So when we lose something, we can still maintain and act like nothing is wrong. That's worth its weight in gold. When you are raised in a higher economic environment, you are judged by your job titles, spouse, house, and cars. And when you lose the title of CEO or something, and the big house is gone, that's when the suicide rate goes up. Three out of ten will not make it after the losses. If you were raised in a poor environment and have to go back, you will feel like you are on familiar ground. That's some deep stuff.

WE ALL TAKE MESS FROM TIME TO TIME.

Even rich people have to answer to someone. Things are not always going to be like we want them to be. I am just telling you if you have to take some mess off someone, make sure it is going to benefit you. Don't just take mess because you are feeling down and somebody has got the best of you. Life is designed for stuff to get in your way. That's why you have to lean on God to give you strength for different things. It is a test to see how you get over one hurdle, so He gives you this other one till you are hurdling to where you need to be. I might be sounding crazy, but if you think about it long enough, you know what I am saying.

THE YEARS CAN GO SO FAST.

I think one of our biggest problems is we don't know how fast the years go. We're so busy taking care of these kids and trying to have a life and enjoy ourselves that the years just sneak up on us. We've got to stop at some point and start thinking that we are getting older too. We can't be eighty years old trying to borrow a hundred dollars. You have got to secure yourself some kind of way where you can make it out of this life and leave something for your kids. Quit playing around with your life. Stop hanging in the clubs and on the streets and in the malls. It seems that everyone thinks you have to try to beat the other person so that you can make it to the destination first. Remember, it doesn't matter how fast you get there, what's important is being there right on time. Have you ever seen somebody pass you and go through ten or fifteen cars, weaving and bobbing, speeding and running lights and by the time he gets to the third light, you are right behind him? What I'm trying to tell you is that you don't have to break any rules and rush to get over there, just head that way. If you are going to rush to anything, by all means, rush to God.

When the Cows Come Home.

My grandmother used to say, "I'm going to wait till the cows come home." I never understood that, but I think it means that she is going to take a little longer to do what she has to do. Well, sometimes the cow doesn't come home. Now the man is just sitting around looking crazy. I am going to take my time to say this: If you are past forty-five and you are still out there playing with someone's life, you should be ashamed of yourself.

Someday I will make this statement on national television, because that is how important it is to me. Let me encourage you to raise your expectations, start seeing yourself for the remainder of your life receiving good things. You ought to expect the favors of God. God has great things for your life. He wants you to enjoy and keep living because the best years are yet to come. I want to tell all women and men, by the time you are forty- five, you should have done most of everything you wished or wanted to do.

By now you should have seriously learned a few things. You should know the difference between good and evil; love and hate. At this age, you ought to be sure of a few things. You should own a few things, like having a financial portfolio. And stop thinking they are asking to see a picture book of your kids. You should be able to tell another young man or woman the dos and don'ts in life. You should be able to affect generations to come and give them a wealth of information, experience, and influence.

At this age, things start happening to the body. If you don't eat, exercise, and live a clean and healthy lifestyle, arthritis becomes your best friend. And then old Arthur brings on high blood pressure and diabetes. The weather starts changing, and asthma and bursitis step in. Please don't forget viruses and the flu. You don't really understand everything that is going on with your body, but you are aware that your body is changing, and it's not what it used to be. I am not a doctor, but you know exactly what I am talking about. I will ask you one question: How are you sick and still playing the game? Great minds will wonder about that one and want to know if you have found an answer.

See, you have to understand that at this age, it is time to prove to someone that you are a very respectful and honest person. You want the other person to know how much you love him and that you would do anything for him. So when it is time for your roll call to go down, you are over there sick and flies are swarming around you, and someone has exchanged your drawers for some Depends diapers. And now you are too weak to pick up the flyswatter to keep the flies off.

You have to understand that you did not put your time in with the person who is trying to show you love. Make sure that you put in the right amount of time. Don't just put in enough to get by, but spend some quality time with the person you love. Go out of your way to do some things. This is a time when you want to go above and beyond your call of duty. Remember the love that you have for your mate.

It is like baking a cake; you have to make sure that you put in all of the right measurements. You have to do all the right things to make the cake perfect. If you don't include all the right ingredients, the cake may not rise at all. And if you don't do your relationship the same way, one of the parties might not rise to the occasion at hand. You might have to redo some things, or maybe even apologize and mean it from the heart, not just words. Really mean it and never do it again. I know that you think some things are really hard, but being a responsible and caring individual will make a person stand by you through the thick and thin, and when life lands you a blow, he or she will make sure to be right beside you to help you stand again.

You can play around if you want to and end up alone or with cancer or heart disease. When you get older, if you built a strong and loving bond with someone, that person doesn't mind taking care of you. This person will care what happens to you. Of course, your mother and father if they are still living will be there, and maybe your sisters and brothers. But we all need that special someone in our life to go all the way with us to the end. So many men have run the streets for so long that by the time you get them, their minds are ready to surrender, but their bodies have already started to break down. Just be prepared in case you end up with a good sick or a good fat man. I was lucky enough to find a wife who cared enough about me to make sure I went to the doctor, because we men are too afraid to go to the doctor alone!

STOP LOOKING AT *DAYS OF OUR LIVES* AND START LOOKING AT *ONE LIFE TO LIVE.*

You have to get out there and make things happen for you. See, if you believe that you will never be anything, that is probably the way you'll be. If you think that you'll be everything, you will definitely be something, and more than likely someone great. Don't accept no for an answer. Believe that you can be whatever you want to and try to achieve all of your goals. It's like remodeling your house. If you change just one thing, you'll have to add something else to go with that change, otherwise your house will look crazy. Your life is the same way and your relationship is the same way. I think one of the reasons why this book thing is working for me with no education is that I did it out of the pureness of my heart. I didn't know what I was doing. I just said I was going to do it. People would say, "What if it doesn't work?" Then I would say to them, "What if it does work?" See, if it doesn't work, I'm going to be right where I am right now. But if it does work, I'm going to make a few steps forward. So I went on and proceeded with my idea of writing a book. And I began to think, "What if the book did what I said it was going to do?" Once again, that's really what this thing is about. Belief and action are the keys to success in life.

You have what it takes to be the best that you can be. You've got the power to achieve the things you desire most. No one can take what you have from you. You are destined to be great. Your success is waiting for you to claim it fully. I know that you are searching for what is holding you back, but I'm here to tell you today that the problem is you. What are you waiting for? Believe me, you can do it!

WHEN YOU FALL, GET BACK UP AND GET IN THE RACE.

You know life has its stumbling blocks where you are going to fall, and your job is to get back up and get back in the race. Sometimes it's even harder to enter the race, because you know you're not fast enough to win it, so you don't want to get in it. But I would advise everyone that if you want to be in the race, whether you lose or win, the big accomplishment is getting in the race. You might win the next time; you never know. The front-runner might have a heart attack, or anything could happen. I'll enter a spelling bee competition knowing I am not a doggone speller. But what if the guy who's in first place chokes and I can spell that word or the next word? The contest might end up a draw.

We all have something we can't do, but we have to push past it, because God gave us a gift we can use. You have to continue to work on those things you can't do. Rome was not built in a day. So you have to take your time and seek knowledge to learn how to do those things that seem as if they're difficult tasks. Practice makes perfect. The longest walk in the world started with just one step. If you are not satisfied with your life, you have to improve. Sooner or later, you will run across your gift. And that is the thing that God put you on this earth to do. The graveyard is full of brand-new gifts that have never been touched before. Make sure you open yours before you die.

Enjoy Your Life, Enjoy Your Moments, and Enjoy Being a Woman!

And most of all don't be scared. You're being flung into a world that's running about as smoothly as a car with square wheels. It's okay to be uncertain. Learning to be positive, confident, and mature is not always easy. Learning to be a woman is even more difficult, and you're not sure you're ready for it. The best way to handle it is just to take it one day at a time. No matter how many books you have read, and how many people you have talked to, you are the only one who knows where you are trying to go. It's like a road map; it can get you to the stand and the street, but you will have to know where your destination lies.

Women Have to Be Nurtured Just Like a Beautiful Flower.

Now that I am helping the ladies, I look at them like flowers that are trying to grow. I'm their Miracle-Gro. Because sometimes you have to nourish the flowers or your petals will fall off. When you are reading this book, it probably makes you think I'm trying to tell you to leave men alone and just be right with God. But I'm just telling you to slow down. You have got to make the morning last. When I go to church, I sit and listen just like you. You can argue about the Bible and God's word all day, because people don't always agree on what they heard. And all I can do is help you understand the way I heard it, to help make sense of it all.

I have not read the entire Bible. All I can do is tell you what I heard. I heard tell that everytime God talks about moving forward, He's talking about walking. I have not heard yet where He took off running anywhere. So that means if you slow down, you'll still get where you are going in the right way. If you are in the same place that you have been all these years and you keep running into the same type of man, something's wrong. You've been running your life the same way for the last five to ten years, and it does not look like anything is changing. Well, you could be growing like a vegetable, but the problem is maybe it's the dirt that you have been growing in. Maybe it's the dirty man you have. Maybe your soil is full of sand, and that is the reason you are not growing into a person.

TAKE YOUR TIME AND USE YOUR HEAD.

I'm a true believer that only fools rush in and only mad people rush out. I'm trying to tell you that anytime you make a decision, slow down and use the right head and right frame of mind and make a concrete, rock-hard decision on what you are going to do. Ask yourself, "Can I live with this decision I've made, or can I live without it?" There you will find the answer.

STOP USING THE WORD "FRIEND" SO LOOSELY.

If you can find one friend in a lifetime, you are a blessed human being. Let's change the word "friends" to "associates," until you investigate the situation. Remember, friends are hard to come by, and if you find a good friend, you certainly want to hold on to him or her. A good friend will be with you to the end. He or she will be with you at the hospital, during the birth of your children, and any other thing that you might need him or her for. You know, there is another friend who will stick closer than a brother, and his name is JESUS. Please don't forget about that one.

To Keep a Secret, You'll Have to Keep It to Yourself.

You know, what's so funny to me is that we tell our best friend a secret and then expect him or her to keep it. What we don't realize is that if the secret was so hot, so juicy that we couldn't help but tell it, how do we expect someone else to keep it? The only way to keep your personal business from getting out is to keep it to yourself.

Speaking of Strength.

I'll tell you about some of the strongest women who made a difference in this game called life. I used the word "game," and my wife asked me, "Is love a game?" I replied, "Yes, because someone is always playing with your heart." I have to truly say that my wife, Hillary Clinton, Cookie Johnson, and Oprah are four of the strongest women in the world as far as I'm concerned. My wife stands by me at all times. Oprah is not faking it. On TV, she stands for what she stands for and doesn't care that she is not married. She is not debating it, and she does not care who says what about it. She is just holding her ground, and that's what womanhood is all about: holding your ground, no matter what people say. You know what you want, you know what you want to do, you know your commitment to yourself, and you know your commitment to your man. So when my wife Lauren, Hillary Clinton and Cookie Johnson said, "I do," I believe they meant it. "For better or for worse, richer or poorer, in sickness and in health"—they meant that, and they are holding their ground. You can call them fools or think they are fools if you want to, but all I see is some strong women. Oprah believes that her life is fine just like it is. She is wide-open and is not keeping it a secret. Maybe you can learn something from these women. As far as I'm concerned, all are powerful women and I commend them.

Do Something Special with Your Love.

If you can't do anything with all the love that God has put in your body for yourself, how are you going to truly love someone else? I'm talking about all the love He gave you just for you. You have messed over it, or thrown it away. You have let other people have your love who didn't deserve it! You give all of it and then some. Do you really know what love is? Love does not harm you! What I'm saying is, learn how to use the love that God has given you and be careful whom you give your love to; every man won't appreciate it. And when you do meet someone special, and he has love and you do too, you can share in each other's love, which makes a beautiful situation.

I am pretty sure that's what is meant when they say "equally yoked." When I met my wife, my love was still like a used car with low mileage, because I was using the word "love" more than the action of love. Because I learned that most of the time all you have to do is say the word "love" to women and they will believe it. As soon as you tell a woman that you love her, she will give you hers so fast to try to catch up with your love that you just lied about. So I figured, why use mine up when I can live off hers? If you are saying to yourself, "That's a dirty suckah," you are finally beginning to understand the true meaning of suckahism. But don't try to teach it to your girlfriends until you have finished reading the book. There are many different angles to a suckah. There are some unknown things about a suckah that even a scientist hasn't discovered. They are doing a brain scan and I think that's the wrong test, because the way suckahs think, they might not have a brain. You know that I am not lying!

IF YOU THINK THIS MESSAGE ISN'T FOR YOU.

When I talk to large crowds, I always talk like there's only one person in the room. I love talking to one person at a time. I really don't have to worry about that, because when I let God speak through me, He is going to hit whoever needs to be hit at that moment. You can be in God's house but in the wrong room. What I mean is that when women hear me talking about men slapping and cheating on them, they holler, "No man has ever done me like that." You are not through living yet, and it can easily happen. If you haven't met him now, you never know whom you will meet down the road. If it hasn't happened to you yet, just be quiet and let the ones it has happened to receive the message.

ARE YOU AFRAID OF THE LIGHT?

You see, sometimes people are scared of the light because in the dark you can sleep your problems away. But in the light you wake up and have to face another day, which means you have to be constructive in your life and make something happen. What you do in the dark will come to the light anyway. God sees you either way. The dark and the light are like Heaven and Hell. It's so easy to go to Hell because it is for people who give up and make excuses to stay down. It's hard to get to Heaven because the expectations are high and you have to rise to the occasion. So are you afraid of the light? You don't owe me an answer, but you owe that one to yourself.

STEP UP AND BECOME A LEADER AT SOMETHING.

I would like to see women who are followers step up to be leaders. Leadership is not hard; it just knows which way to go. No one wants to step in those shoes, because they seem so big. But if you would just step out of yourself sometimes and step into the real life that God has created for you, you'll find out that you are more than you thought you were. Once you find what you are really supposed to be in life, you won't want to step back. There's something really attractive about a person with purpose, drive, and determination. Just remember that when you get your power, try to help someone else get his or hers.

Twelve

God

WHEN YOU NEED DIRECTION, READ YOUR BIBLE.

My grandmother used to cook for a living and she taught me a lot about baking. One thing she always told me was to quit guessing what to throw in the pot. If you're stuck on something or you have doubts, just go back to the book and it will tell you exactly what to put in the cake. It made sense to me. When I needed direction, I went back to the Bible, and it taught me how to bake a different kind of cake. You put in a teaspoon of roughness, just a teaspoon, enough to add a little edge. Put in four cups of sugar, just to add a little sweetness to the cake. Then I added some flowers, which I gave to her. I turned the heat up to 350 and she told me, "Now, you are cooking with gas." I knew it was not a mistake when I ate a piece of that cake.

Some people think using the box of cake mix is a better way. The problem we have today is that nobody wants to bake from scratch anymore. Everybody wants to put the box in there, add a couple of eggs and some water, and think his or her life is going to be just fine. We've got to go back to old school and bake it from scratch. That way, you'll know exactly what ingredients you put in it. You'll know exactly how it's supposed to taste at the end. Quit relying on the Betty Crocker cake mix. Making a homemade cake is like washing your body; you may have to go the long way around to keep it clean. You have to do a little extra work to make it worth your while. Writing this book has really given me a lot of respect for the Bible. You could read this book one time. If it gets boring, you may put it down. You might tell one or two of your girlfriends about it. But that Bible is something! It's been on the bestseller list forever!

GIVE THE POWER TO GOD.

Women, stop letting men overpower you and give the power back to the person who controls all the power, who gave it to mankind, who gave it to the world, and that is God. We keep trying to get away from what God says. We want to go by what we say. It's funny how you run your whole life in a circle and what you really need is right there before your eyes. We will run our own way. We forget about what He gave us and try to create our own stuff, but we always come back home. You know, I guess life is about going out and making mistakes. When you finally find yourself, I guess you could say you really found something. But I know one thing: You can see God now, or you can see Him later, but sooner or later you are going to see Him.

GOD KNOWS.

I've been so stupid in my life thinking, "If I don't go to church, or if I don't praise God, He won't know what I'm doing, and I can get away with misusing and mistreating women." Silly me. He knew all the time, but He guided me through my whole life to get me to where I am today, where I can share and help someone with my so-called ignorance. I can help women because of the things I've caused in other people's lives.

God has done a wonderful thing for me. He let me see through a rich person's eyes just how good life can be. And all the wonderful things that He has created that some people will never experience, like living in a lavish hotel, riding in private jets, fishing from and dining on luxurious yachts, and going on shopping sprees buying one-of-a-kind shoes and suits. But even with all that I have seen, I am still able to remain levelheaded and be myself, because it is not my money. It belongs to the rich people. But there is no doubt in my mind that I am a wealthy man because I have God. With God first in my life, the riches and the blessings have already started pouring down on me. And as these blessings continuing to overtake me, I still want to remain a blessed man with a level head.

I'm Headed for Heaven; Keep Hell Out of the Way.

I once heard Louis Farrakhan say that "a man would have to be a fool to want to lead the people, but once you are called you have no choice." Now I understand what he meant, because people hold a magnifying glass and a hearing aid to everything you say and do. Usually it is the people who never do anything to help someone else. I guess that is why they have plenty of time to harass you.

Since I have changed my outlook on life, I try to do the right things as best as I know how. I am not saying that I am holier than thou, and I don't call myself a saint, but I am an honest man and I will tell the truth and tell you off at the same time. That is why I am begging you to please keep Hell out of my way. If God had something He considered His worst, I would still take that because it will be something better than anything that I could ever imagine. So don't push me, because I'm close to the edge. I am still headed for Heaven, but Hell keeps knocking on my door asking me, "Can Boom come out to play?"

I DON'T BELIEVE IN ZODIAC SIGNS.

Some women are so tied up trying to find out what sign a man is that they look over the sign that is staring them in the face, letting them know that something is not right. You think because he is a certain sign that you have found Mr. Right. You say, "Oh, we're compatible." Then you date him for only three weeks and he is gone. You try to make sure that he fits your personality while you are overlooking reality.

There is no real way to tell if he is a good man, but if he is being good, ride it out as long as you can. Pay attention to some of his signs and actions, because actions speak louder than words. Just visit the situation like it's your doctor—check on it every now and then. You know that you have to visit the doctor so many times a year, so make sure that you are checking in on your man more than once a year. Make sure that he treats you like you would treat a tooth. If you don't take care of it, you will lose it.

WHEN YOU LOSE SOMEONE YOU LOVE.

When you lose someone you love, whether it is divorce or death, remember that a man may be watching and waiting for the right time to approach the situation. His job is to be there for you in the time of need, when you are at your lowest point. He will try to bring joy and laughter into your heart, to stroke your heart, rub your back, and give you plenty of hugs. He will take you places so that he can take your mind off of the loss you have encountered. At this time he wants to please you any way he can, which moves him closer in finding out information about you. He wants to know what you have left to give and what you have coming your way. This is a dangerous and slick man who knows his way around. Right now, this man is making you feel so secure that you feel like you are coming back to reality. You certainly don't want to lose him at this point, which leaves you giving anything to keep him. That is the beginning of another loss.

Losing a loved one hurts so bad that you will do anything to get rid of the pain. But putting your life in a stranger's hands can only devastate you even more. The best thing to do is to talk to friends and loved ones and people you know who have crossed that path before. Every person has a different recovery rate. Never let anyone rush you into thinking you can make the pain disappear, because it will only come back twice as hard, because you can't hide love. I heard a preacher say, "Love and pain cannot reside in the same body at the same time." Something will give! But I found that helping someone who is worse off than I am is another way to bring my spirit up. And you have to realize your loved one is in a better place. The hardest part of this journey is holidays or seeing someone you both loved and enjoyed being around. So work on your mind, because your heart is stronger than you think. It can replenish itself, but your mind is a terrible thing to lose.

LET'S PRAY.

The next time a man talks you into the bedroom, try to see what he would do in an awkward situation. Get half naked and hold both of his hands and look him in the eye and say, "Let's pray." And let him lead the prayer. Leave your eyes open and watch his response. He'll either tell you, "I'm not doing that, are you crazy?" or he'll want it so bad that he will begin to pray. I know that I am talking to myself, because many of you would never do this because it might scare you out of the bedroom and mess up your thrill.

But that is what is wrong with the world, so many people are scared to take chances. But you have to remember one thing: You can't lose what you never had, but you can win something that wants you. The only time you lose is when you don't want it. Be careful what you ask for.

HELP PULL SOMEONE UP.

We have to start reaching back and pulling somebody up. All of us have to take the responsibility to teach somebody what we know is right. We're all guilty of it. Who am I to have knowledge and know the difference between right and wrong, and not share it with someone who doesn't know? Now the bigger question is: Who are you? You can help just like I can, but you refuse to because you don't want anybody in your space. It is not your space. We are here for just a little while. We are borrowing this space, and we are going to have to share it with someone else. My life is moving forward because I'm trying to help people. You can't be in your own little world trying to praise God but not helping anyone else.

I would help people not knowing the importance of what I was doing. I call that having fun. When I lived in Oklahoma, I bought a four-wheel drive so that I could help stranded people when snowstorms came through, which was often. There would be people in ditches and I would drive around and see who was stuck and pull them out. Most of them would be nervous women who were stranded. They got caught in the storm coming home from work. I would give them my phone number just in case they needed something else. I can hear you saying again, "That suckah just won't quit." But I'm asking you, which one would you rather have? Your car stuck in the ditch or your car on the road with a phone number you can always throw away?

GIVE MORE AND RECEIVE MORE!

The more you give on earth, the more you will receive in Heaven. Why don't you make it easier for yourself where you're going to be for eternity? No one cares about you when you are old and on this earth. Once you reach seventy or eighty years old, you are left all alone because people believe, "If I lend a seventy-year-old person some money, when is she going to pay me back? What if she dies before she pays me back?" So they don't pay attention to the older people. They just leave them sitting over there in wheelchairs and rocking chairs, not realizing there is knowledge in old people that is beneficial. I don't care if they don't pay you back. If they can tell you a few things to help you along the way, that is your payback. They can help you get along with your life. If it isn't money, we don't think it is payback because we let money determine how our lives are supposed to go. You don't understand how much just simple words can affect a person's life. I know, because a few simple words changed my life. You should talk to everybody. I don't care if you don't think they aren't listening to you.

One thing about people: They might play like they don't hear you, but they hear you. And every now and then you might say something that means something to someone. I have plenty of people come tell me, "You remember that time you told me this or that? I want you to know that changed my life." I don't remember saying it, but they do. So I am telling you that it has a lot to do with the words you hear. What makes it mean something to you is when you believe in the person who said it. So why don't you be that special someone in someone else's life?

When You're Nervous, Go to Church and Take Your Kids.

If you are nervous about making changes in your life, go to church. Take your kids with you, so that their road won't be so long and hard. Quit waiting for your man to wake up and lead you to church every Sunday. You didn't come into the world with him and you are leaving here without him. I don't care if you die in the same accident; you'll still go your separate ways. They might bury you beside each other, but I have never seen a double casket. Men are funny. If you leave them alone and do what you have to do, after you go to church without him a few Sundays, he'll beat you getting dressed. Another thing, quit letting your kids just run around stupid, because stupid kids end up being stupid grown-ups, and we all know a few. Quit telling them to sit down and shut up. They might have something to say. They might be developing themselves to be something great, but we shut them down quickly, so we can get some quiet time or look at our favorite TV show. But where can you find a good clean television show these days? I have seen them kissing on cartoons.

If People Pray Together, They Stay Together.

It doesn't always work, and maybe the reason is that God knows one of you is not sincere about your prayer. Stop thinking you can fool God like you do your mate. Just remember one thing: He made you and He knows your heart. It sure does help when couples go to church together and pray and worship the Lord. You leave church holding hands and smiling, and laughter fills your soul and you feel like you can conquer the world.

But, ohhh, comes Monday, all hell breaks loose. It could be because you are back to your everyday life. The workload and the pressure are back in full force and effect. I have a solution: Quit waiting until Sunday to pray. People act like it is against the law to pray more than once a week. I did, until I met my wife. We have to say a prayer before we eat. I was not accustomed to prayer and was afraid to do it publicly. I thought that it was something to do when you are in trouble. I didn't know you could pray anywhere, anytime, or anyplace. Once I learned the power of prayer, I learned about the power in me, which gave me the strength to try to help instill the power in you and help you to know the power of love.

NEVER GIVE UP.

Channel your energy in a positive direction. Stop worrying God and your friends, because negative energy attracts negative men. When you find out how to channel the energy, it will happen for you. You can't want it so badly that you will do anything for it. When you do that, you end up in the middle of nowhere. Relax and find something else to do with your time and just try to help somebody else with the energy you are using trying to find somebody. The right person will come out of nowhere 'cause God hears it and He sees you. You just don't think He does. You feel like He's taking too long. You can't ask God for a man and then turn around in the same breath and say, "He's probably not going to do it." Remember, faith is the answer.

TALK TO GOD LIKE HE'S YOUR BEST FRIEND.

I see people who talk to God in their own little world, and they get better results than you do. Just get up and talk to Him like he is your best friend. These people get a lot more blessings. See, it's one thing to go in there and read the Bible and shout amen and all that, then go through the day without really believing that there is a God. There are plenty of you like that. All I do is talk to God and tell Him where I'm trying to go in my life and praise Him for the way He has my life going now. It seems like He just keeps lifting me up because I'm putting in a 100 percent effort in my life every day. I mean, He has always been there for me, I just didn't know it was Him working. I thought it was just me. You know, I wasn't giving Him credit for it, but now I know that it is not me. God and I are fighting together against the world, changing lives inch by inch. Now we are on the buddy-buddy system.

TALK TO GOD AND FACE YOURSELF.

If you're confused at this point in your life, I think there are only two people you need to talk to. The first is God and the second is in that mirror you look into every morning to see what you see. If you talk to God and that mirror, pretty soon you will see someone different, because confessions are good for the soul. If you tell God all the things you are dealing with, He knows how to bring comfort to your soul. If you keep looking at yourself in the mirror, you might not like what you see, and you will have no choice but to change it for the betterment of your mind, body, and soul. You must search your soul and listen to what God is saying to you. He may be requiring something different from you. That is why you have to consult with Him, because He may be taking you down a different avenue so that you can get to your place in Him.

God may require a few basic principles from His followers, but those who have a certain kind of calling may have to do certain things. God may send you through a few challenges and hardships to see what you are made of. Of course, He already knows, but you have to be sure. Because when you are faced with oppositions, you have to know that God is a deliverer and He will bring you out no matter how dim the situation looks.

As you began to read many stories in the Bible, there is one in particular where Jesus was getting ready to die on the cross for mankind. He was asking God to let the bitter cup pass from him, but I guess Jesus thought about it and said, "Let thy will be done." I am sure at that point in time he felt rejected and neglected, but he believed in his father enough to know that in the end, everything would be all right. And as our children believe in us, they have to know that we have their best interests at heart, especially when you are a parent who is not running the streets and you are trying to protect and care for your children.

SO MUCH MORE TO LIFE.

As you are living this life, you may think that the odds are against you. But believe me, there is so much more to life that you could be doing. You have to find your passion in life and your reason for existing. You have to believe in who you are are and then you have to rely and depend on a higher source. Yes, we know that life can knock us off our feet at times, but we also know that there are other times when we feel like we are on the mountaintop. What is your passion? What do you love to do? How do you plan on doing it? You really have to know these things, so that you can follow in the path that God is leading you. Never leave a stone unturned. You may end up doing one thing you like, and it may lead you into something you love. You might not have known your full potential, but here you are now, loving what you do. Someone may ask you, "How did you get involved in that?" Sometimes you may not have a clear explanation of how it all happened, you just know that it did. Sometimes, a person may have just one thing that she is good at, and ventures off into other things and finds out that she is a genius at that new thing that was discovered. You are unique and created by the Almighty. There will be some victories in your life that you will live to tell about. You will have some good experiences and some bad ones too, but I know that the good ones are going to outweigh the bad ones. Look at where I come from. Who would have thought that I would change my life? See, you never know if you don't take that chance.

I have had many of struggles along the way, and some failures too. But I have had some triumphs as well. I have a wife who dearly loves me. Not only does she care about me physically but mentally. She wants to make sure that I have a personal relationship with God. She wants to make sure that I am eating the Word of God properly and digesting it. She cares about my safety. I care about her as well. I have had some women in my life who I knew didn't care anything about me. But look at what I have now. I am pleased with who I am and pleased with whom I have working on my side: God, my wife, and my family. If you allow Him to put people like this in your life, there is no telling what you can do. Open up your heart to receive, because He comes in many ways, and He is not limited to how and whom He can move through. And that is why opening up is so important, so that you don't miss the opportunity that He sends your way.

A FOOLISH DREAMER.

As you are sitting by watching the time go by, don't sit in the corner and dream your life away. Dreaming is good, but you can't stay in that position forever. After the dream is over, you have to get up and do something about it. Some dreams never come alive, because some people never do anything about them. What are you dreaming about? Some people have bad dreams, and they never want them to come to life, but then there are those good ones, where you can see yourself doing exactly what you see in your dream. When is it going to happen? one might ask. I don't have any idea, but I know that you have to get up off your seat of "do nothing" and get moving. You have to take a step and move forward if you want things to change and happen in your life.

Foolish dreamers wait until the last minute to do anything. They feel as if they have plenty of time on their hands, not thinking that life will pass them by. You have to take the opportunity as it comes and not put it off for a rainy day. Foolish dreamers sit by the side of the road and watch the cars go by, thinking that one day they will own one, but never plan to get a job so that they can have a stable income. Time keeps on going when everything else is standing still. Have you ever noticed that time keeps on going even when yours runs out? It keeps right on ticking. So I would advise you to get up and start ticking and start your journey, because time waits for no one, regardless of the excuses that we may have. Time doesn't understand them!

THE MAIN ISSUE.

One of the main issues we see demonstrated over and over again is people's lack of vision. What do they see? You know in a natural sense, if you are having eye problems, you can hardly see anything. In a real sense, if you do not have a "vision" for your life, you will end up twiddling your thumbs, not knowing where to go. It is like being in a field and looking around and wondering, "How did I get here?" You must have a vision, because without a vision, you will perish. You must have a destination in mind, and you need to have a sense of purpose.

What goals have you set for yourself? Where do you see yourself in the future? If you don't own a house now, do you plan to in the near future? If so, how long is it going to take you to get the finances you need to own one? What kind of preparations have you made? Or do you believe in making any at all? Do you think that things are going to drop in your lap? What kind of planet are you living on? You have to prepare for things to take place. Investors and stockbrokers don't put all their money in one stock; they put a little here and a little there. Never put all your eggs in one basket. Open your eyes so that you can see what is going on around you. And to get a larger view of what is happening around the world, read the newspaper and look at the news. You might not have to go that far; just look at your next-door neighbors. What are they doing to branch out and extend their views and quality of life? Go to some of the local colleges and check out what programs they have that will fit into your schedule. You might be surprised by all of the new class schedules and their flexibility in working with people from all walks of life. Things are changing, you know. Day by day, you have to keep up with what's going on in your world. Stay focused and make sure that you are keeping eyedrops in your eyes so that you can see the vision in front of you.

DO YOU SEE WHAT I SEE?

There is a movie called *Akeelah and the Bee,* and one of the things that Akeelah says in this movie is, "It is not that we are inadequate, but we are adequate beyond measure." Now, isn't that something. Do you know what is on the inside of you? Do you know exactly what you are made of? I know that you have genes from both sides of your family, but which ones are dominant? Is there one that is more dominant than the other? Sometimes, a person can just look at you and say, "Wow, have you ever thought about doing this or that?" And you respond by saying, "No, I don't think that I can do that." Well, why not take a chance on that? If other people see it, you might want to take a look at it. Because we are so hard on ourselves, we won't push forward to do that thing in our heart. But you have to, because you will never know if you never try. And again, it is okay to fail once or twice; just get back up and dust your feet off and keep on trying.

Have you ever thought about how many times teachers and principals have taken their exams? You might want to ask them. One of my friends told me that she used to substitute in a certain school district, and she would hear them saying that they had taken tests seven or eight times, and they finally passed. So I am saying that it is not always going to be easy, but if you persist and persevere, I guarantee that you will succeed. You may even dream about passing or doing something outstanding, but it will happen if you don't give up. The key thing is to keep trying. You won't be the first person who failed, and certainly you won't be the last.

Don't be afraid to dream big. If you see yourself with large sums of money and being prosperous and successful, there is certainly nothing wrong with that. You have to see yourself doing things, and it is okay if it is something big. Some people will get arrogant and proud and thinking that they are better than others. Be careful about this one, because it takes only one car wreck or one handicap to put everything back into perspective for you. Always reach back to get someone else. You can always appreciate where you came from. If you keep the circle going, it will continue to grow, and people from all walks of life will benefit because you cared enough to reach out and reach back. You will be glad you did! Your blessings will continue to flow.

GO FORTH AND SHINE.

In the church world there is a song that says, "This little light of mine, I'm going to let it shine . . . everywhere I go, I'm going to let it shine." Even if it is a little light, such as a smile, let it go with you everywhere. If you are smiling, most of the time you are full of joy and people can hear it in your voice, on the telephone, when you are typing on the computer, and everything else that you touch, people will feel it. There is nothing wrong with letting the world know how much joy you have on the inside, even when things are going wrong. Don't let circumstances pull you out of the light and get in your way of helping someone else's light to shine.

People will see that glow in you and wonder, "What is going on in her world? She must have hit the lottery or something for her to walk around with a glow like that." You didn't tell them that your car just broke down and someone broke into your house. You didn't share with them that you just lost your job and your mother just died. But you keep on smiling because the light is shining so brightly on the inside that it is bursting loose on the outside.

Thank God that everyone does not have to handle the same situations. Some people are good at funerals, and others just can't take it. Some people can console others and help them to get back to their life. Others may feel that their life is over after a tragedy or a death. But the light that shines in others can help restore you and make you whole again. That is why it is important to know your calling, because people need you. There are missionaries and people who love to visit hospitals, but there are others who can't stand the smell and throw up every time they enter a hospital room. Your calling and mine may be different, but I guarantee we can use both of them effectively.

When I go into a bank or grocery store, it brings me joy to see the banker and the tellers smiling. I am sure there is a story behind the smiles, but the smiles just brighten up my day. When I am talking to people, I always try to smile and bring laughter and joy into the situation. I want to create a joyous presence in the room. Although bad things may have happened that day, I want people to know that there is still hope, so keep on smiling and keep letting that little light shine. It is okay if it is small; it will get bigger over time and the world will see it as well. Then, everywhere you go, you will smile, and others will smile back at you. As you go up and down the street, let it shine all over the world. Keep the little light burning!

DOES ANYBODY UNDERSTAND?

When you are at a crucial point in your life and you are wondering if anybody understands where you are coming from, some people will understand and some won't. Not everybody has had some of the same experiences as you have. So maybe their world and experiences are different. But I will tell you one person who will understand, and that is God. He knows what is in your heart. He knows what you have been through and where you are going. He even knows how you are going to come out of the situation you are in. You just have to believe that He understands.

Have you ever met someone in your life who had a bad past but now is living the good life? Sometimes these people forget where they came from. They forget about the times that they robbed, lied to, and stole from individuals. They even forget that they were on crack cocaine so bad that they could not lift their heads up, but they don't want others to know just how bad they really were. Then all of a sudden, someone reminds them of who they were and what they did in the past. There is always someone lurking around who knows all about you. So don't be afraid to let people know where you have been or where you are now. You are not going to stay in that position forever. You will move on to something else. It does take time.

If people began to share some of their sadness and pain they have endured in life, this would help others to overcome things they think are hopeless. If you have older siblings, you might want to ask them about their lives and what they did and how they overcame such things. If you have none, ask other family members and friends. Of course, you don't want to take the advice of everyone, but do take some advice. Some of the local churches have all kinds of programs going on. Join one of the programs to help you overcome your situations. There are people who have faced and still are facing some hard situations, but they keep on reaching because they know that a better day is coming and things are going to get better. It might not seem like it, but it will. Yes, there are people who understand where you are coming from. I am a man who has experienced many things in my life and has done many things, and if I can change and things can work for me, I know they can for you too. I am a witness to that!

REACH FOR MY HAND AND DON'T LET IT GO.

Hold my hand and don't let it go. Feel the pain. So many people in the world need someone to hold their hand and make them a part of their lives. They are in a place in their life that they have never been in before and they are confused, because they have thought that life was a certain way and things were always going to be good for them, but now they have found out differently. They need a friend and a confidant to stand and walk beside them. They want to know that everything is going to be all right. Although confusion has taken over their mind and soul, they want to keep on believing that all is well. They don't want to give up on God and their belief. They just need someone to be that pillar of strength so that they can get through all of this confusion.

When you get to this point in your life, you need a friend to help you process all of this. Because it seems that everything you thought was real is now fantasy. You need people to help pull you up into the right kind of thinking, because your thinking is definitely off. You know what your momma taught you and what the church has taught you, but none of it makes any sense right now. Although you know there is a supreme God, you may even wonder, "If there is a God, where is He?" He is there watching you. He is going to send someone along the way to help lift your spirit so that you can fly. You had to experience what it is like being in the valley. Now you can tell others that they too can come out. And you will have a personal testimony of how He bought you out.

It is kind of funny that when you have your own experiences, you can tell your story with a little more enthusiasm. People will believe you, because some of them have seen you at the lowest, and now you are at your highest peak. People will believe what you tell them, and they will say, "If she came out, I know I can." This is how we are going to change the world and take on the challenges that face us each and every day. We are going to see people change and see them develop into what God has designed for their lives.

DON'T LOSE THE LESSON.

I am sure at some point in everyone's life, they have asked "Why?" Even children have asked why their mother or father is the way he or she is. "How come I couldn't have a different one?" If you were raised poor and grew up in an environment where you didn't have much of anything, you will tend to question that too. But have you ever asked, "Why not me?" You may be one of those big-time talk show hosts one day. Maybe you had to go through many things so that you will have a diverse group of people watching you. Maybe, in the end, it will all work out for your good.

When you are facing your obstacles, don't lose the lesson that you are supposed to learn. Keep your ears and your eyes open.

Listen to what others are saying. Listen to their stories and how they overcame the ghetto and other problems. Who was there to help guide them along the way? Sometimes it is an unrelated person who reaches back to give you the instructions that you need. Wisdom comes in all sizes, shapes, and colors.

THIRTEEN

Your Heart Still Beats: Our Foundation

OUR FOUNDATION WILL HELP THE NEEDY.

I just want to make a note that our foundation will be set up for battered women. It's really for the needy, not the greedy. Don't come faking like something's wrong and it is not, 'cause my wife and I will investigate, and we will find out the truth. The foundation's name has already been registered as Your Heart Still Beats. Of course, my wife will be working right beside me, and she will be the director of our foundation. We believe if you give the wrong man your heart, don't give him the beat. If he leaves you with a broken heart, your beat will still be strong enough to pump blood into your heart and you will be able to survive.

OUR MISSION.

Your Heart Still Beats Foundation is a nonprofit agency dedicated to promoting personal growth for women seeking self-sufficiency. Our program provides the tools that raise self-esteem, promote ethics, and build the confidence necessary to succeed in the workplace.

- Expands the traditional job-training curriculum to include positive self-image, appropriate workplace behavior, and appearance
- Helps clients build self-confidence by identifying personal barriers for inner growth and developing a positive self-concept
- Offers workshops focused on recognizing personal worth, practicing effective communication skills, and establishing consistent work ethics
- Provides image consulting to help clients select professional clothing and accessories for the workplace from Your Heart Still Beats Foundation

We welcome new or nearly new

- contemporary interview-appropriate skirts and pantsuits
- attractive, crisp blouses
- beautiful business casual separates
- trousers, dress pants, skirts, blazers, jackets
- professional maternity and junior wear
- sharp, stylish jewelry, handbags, and scarves
- panty hose—any size or skin tone (new only, please)

We cannot currently accept

- used cosmetics
- used panty hose
- men's clothing
- children's clothing

We request that all donations be

- appropriate for the workplace
- on hangers (rather than in bags or boxes)
- cleaned and pressed
- free of strong odors (mothballs, smoke, body odor)

We serve typically single mothers with little personal or financial support. Many are receiving public assistance and the rest fall into the category of the working poor. They are diverse in age, education, ethnicity, and goals. These women have had their opportunities for personal growth limited by a variety of issues including abuse, generational poverty, addiction, and physical disabilities. Many are already working with other agencies to improve their education and skill levels. All of our clients are eager to create a better life for themselves and their children.

FOURTEEN

Closing Remarks

There is so much more in life that you can do, but you decide that you are going to stay right where you are and not move forward. All you want to do is pay your bills, but is that the most important thing in the world? Of course, I realize that you have to do that in order to live. My grandmother told me, "There is no fool like an old fool." And many of us will die that old fool, because we never reach out to do anything else and we act like we care only about what we are doing at that moment. We tell ourselves that we are satisfied, and that is a bad place to be. There is a problem if you are satisfied: When do you get off your behind and do the work that God has put you on this earth to do? Because when it is time to go, you'll be the first person at the gate, hollering, "Can I speak to Him, because y'all don't understand? Let me explain my story." Some people think that if they have a color TV, an apartment, and a car, that's cool. What is that compared to what you can have? I once heard Bishop T.D. Jakes say, "God doesn't get mad about us having stuff. He gets mad, because stuff has us."

The killing thing is that everyone is dressed up nice, and everyone is playing his or her part acting like a big shot. And most of us are a check away from being broke. That's what you call fake it until you make it. Everyone is not going to make it.

You know, what really helped me is when I found out that there were people on the street with college degrees begging for dimes. That stopped me from being ashamed of not having to ask for one and never finishing high school. That really stopped me! I look at what I'm doing with no education, but I have determination, willpower, and a strong drive. And then I look at other people who have college degrees but they are working flipping burgers. And that goes to show you, it may have a little to do with education, but most of it is inside of you. There are a couple of places you can go to get the information or to get what you need. I can think of two places very quickly that can give you the answers and directions on how to get to the place where you need to make it. It is not reaching for the next man, or asking someone to give you a lift to help you get up. One of them is right there in your heart, and the other one is reaching toward the sky, which will make you drop to your knees, and ask Him, "Lord, what must I do, and which way should I go?" You would be surprised at what that will do.

If you start inch by inch, it will slowly turn into step by step. Well, you know, I really started thinking about that. I thought about all the things that I would have to go through to write this book with no education, but I took the first step. I bought a tape recorder and I started recording. After I started recording the words, I knew that I needed to hire someone to write the words and put everything in the proper order and context. I look at things like you are going up a stairway. At first when you are starting to climb it, you count each step. And once you stay in the house for a long period of time, you are able to walk down the stairway without even looking down. Sometimes you come down speeding, because someone is at the door. You haven't looked down once, but you didn't miss a step. That is how easy it is if you only keep stepping. And all I try to do is paint a pretty picture so that you can see exactly what I'm talking about.

And that is what has helped me along the way. I don't only talk; I want you to see what I am saying. I have used my talking skills throughout life to help land me where I needed to go. When I was a young man in the streets, I played like I was a pimp and ended up with prostitutes. I know now that wasn't a good thing. I got older, I played like I had a business, and ended up with several businesses. During the time I was making all that money, I played like I was a bodyguard and ended up working in security for a number of movie stars.

You see, what I'm trying to tell you is that it starts in the mind. You know that we have been told that a mind is a terrible thing to waste. And now that I've gotten older, I said I was a speaker, which has brought me to where I am now. And the only reason I played like I was one is that I told myself this is something I would like to do. And I presented myself that way. Evidently it worked, because I am speaking to you right now. I even dressed the part. But every day that I wake up, I put in 100 percent toward whatever it is I say that I am or say that I am going to do. And someone else happened to see what I am about and helped me to get to where I am today. So sometimes you have to say what you want in order to start heading in that direction to what you want to be and what you want to accomplish. A lot of times, our problem is that we say it, but we don't do anything about it. It all starts with a thought. We need to start thinking about how we are going to change some things that can help us and our family to reach our goals.

You know, the funny thing about me having so many businesses is I really didn't know what I was doing at first. I followed the same principle in all of them, and that is giving my all to the business, and that automatically made me the leader.

Maybe I can share with you the things that have worked for me. It is not about brownnosing and kissing behinds; it's really about creating something that stands out from the rest. Make them feel like if they get rid of you, there is going to be a problem, because no one puts out the work like you, or no one notices the small key elements like you do. You have to find something that no one else is doing, and do it well. Companies will find a way to keep you, even when they let everyone else go.

I grew up watching a lot of TV. I was always in and out of the house. A commercial that I remember seeing was, "A mind is a terrible thing to waste." So I constantly went through the house repeating this. But I realized after I got older that I never did see the ending of the commercial. Once I changed and started searching for God, it let me see the ending of that commercial in a new way. I finally got to see the ending about wasting my mind, and I thought about that. All those years, I had wasted my mind on different things, especially things that were useless.

I had a lady to introduce me one time, and I was looking around for the person that she was talking about, only to find out that she was talking about me. She believed in me more than I did myself. I have asked God many times about my life and to help me. By now, I'm sure He is saying, "Here he comes again." I should have been asking God to give me those eyes that the young lady had that saw the things that she saw about me. Maybe if I had her eyes, I could see the same things too.

You can start on the path to changing your life by admitting that something is wrong with you, rather than continuing to tell people that something is wrong with everyone else. I will listen to people trying to get help every day, because I know that they are reaching out and trying to make their situation better. At this point I may be able to help you or, if not, at least I can offer some suggestions.

I want men to look beyond me messing up their game and at how this could be helping their daughter, sister, or mother. Women sometimes go through things that they don't share with others. They might share it with a girlfriend, but she has to be pretty special. There's a slim chance that she doesn't want to share it with her. Once again, please don't hate me for writing this kind of book. It might help one of your loved ones out of a horrible situation.

For the ladies who are really trying 100 percent, giving all they have, I want to encourage you not to lose faith. When a man finds a good woman before his time, he creates a fairy tale. He puts you in the house, buys you a new car, and gives you the checkbook, and trusts you enough to make you the mother of his kids. He'll keep playing our game on the side, because he is not ready to settle down completely. So he'll go to be with the girlfriend, and race back to the house to check on you. Between the ripping and the running, his game falls weak. So your radar is up that something is just not right. So the first time you catch him, it breaks half your heart. The second time you catch him, it breaks you apart. Now he has completely destroyed the best thing that ever happened to him. We as men will find you and beg for a new start. But reply, "No, I have just read the Bodyguard for Women's Hearts." So say your good-byes and give him my regards. There is life after death, if you keep a pure heart. Just keep on living. I hope you have gotten your life together, and there will be someone else.

Give all that you have to the man or woman of your dreams, because if you do that, he or she will help you to make all your dreams come true. They will be there when needed, to keep you from falling. There are some good men and some good women still running this race. Keep on running to see what the end is going to be. I hope it will be a lifetime of happiness.

Appendix

QUESTIONS

In this section, you'll find a list of questions about both yourself and your relationship. Be honest and answer them to the best of your memory. They can be a means by which you will be able to self-reflect and begin your new life.

1. What is a thing about you that you want people to know that they don't already know?
2. What is it that you feel people don't understand about you?
3. Who do you think people think you really are?
4. If you could have something to enhance your life, and it isn't money or another person, what would it be?
5. What do you need to really help you get ahead in life?
6. What do you plan to do on this earth to improve yourself before you die?
7. What is the biggest secret you are ashamed of that you're keeping from everyone you know?
8. Who is responsible for the one thing that you think is holding you back from getting to where you want to be in life?
9. Do you think you are holding yourself back?
10. Is someone at your job keeping you from climbing the corporate ladder?

11. If so, how are you going to overcome it?

12. What do you call success?

13. Are you successful?

14. What are your plans for the future?

15. What are you going to share with the man of your dreams?

16. Have you found the man of your dreams?

17. Are you in a good place right now?

18. Is life really good to you now?

19. What has the past been like for you?

20. Who is the one person you will feel honored to have bless your life and your relationship?

TEST 1

1. Who is the person who has been there with you the most, meaning going all the way with you?

2. Was he always there (I mean after he let you down a couple of times or didn't show up)?

3. Guess who has never let you down.

4. Guess who has always been there for you.

5. Who has been there for you when the kids were sick?

6. Who was there when you did not think the children were going to make it and you had a hard time believing things would work out?

7. When you had an accident in your car, who was there?

8. Guess who was there when your man left you.

9. Who was there when you couldn't pay for your car?

10. Guess who was there when that man left you crying all night long and you could not pay your bills.

11. Guess who is the one and only man.

If you don't know who this man is at the end of this test, I believe you will have some difficult days ahead. Out of all you have ever done, he has been there for you and he's with you right now even though you aren't with him. You should know the answer, but if you don't, you are in trouble. I'm talking about Jesus, the son of God.

TEST 2

Answer yes or no.

1. Didn't you kind of sense that he had someone else?
2. Can you just stop by his house without calling first?
3. Did your kids tell you that they don't like him?
4. Did your dog growl at him when he came in the house?
5. Did he expect something when he came through the door?
6. Would you let him come back again?
7. Did he leave a good impression with you?
8. Did you think that he was impressed with you?
9. When the man raised his hand and hit you the first time and told you that he would never do it again, did you believe him?
10. Do you believe that there is someone better waiting for you?

If all these answers are yes, why in the world are you sitting there waiting for this man?

TEST 3

1. Name five things you like about him.
2. Name five things you don't like about him.
3. Name his favorite color.
4. Name the color he hates.
5. Name three things he has committed to in the last year.
6. Name one thing about him that everyone keeps warning you about.
7. Name five things he loves about you.
8. Name five things he hates about you.
9. Name all of his children.
10. Name all of his sisters and brothers.

TEST 4

1. What brought you two together?
2. What are you most proud of in your relationship?
3. What goals have you two set for your life?
4. Whom do you blame for not meeting these goals?
5. Describe the ideal marriage.
6. How do you feel a man is supposed to treat his wife?
7. How do you feel a woman is supposed to treat her husband?
8. Which one of you is the better financial manager?
9. What do you feel the role of the woman is?
10. What do you feel the role of the man is?

After you have completed all these tests, take a good look at yourself. It should give you a hint as to what road you are headed down, or if there is a light at the end of the tunnel. I hope that you have answered all the questions honestly. These tests, I believe, will help you grow naturally and spiritually.

WHAT DO MEN WANT?

A survey recently asked what attribute people most associated with being poor and unsuccessful. The top answer was being overweight and the second was smoking.

Women often tell me that men confuse them and that they are unsure what men are really looking for. They have tried to please their men in the past and it hasn't worked. What I advise women to do after they have worked so hard to please their men is to stop and let him start pleasing you. If the media is to be believed, many women don't care what a man is looking for anymore because they have been empowered by their own sexuality and are comfortable in their new role as sexually liberated career women in charge of their own destiny. In which case, as long as the man wants them, that is fine.

It doesn't matter whether that view is actually true or not. What is true is that the modern man is increasingly struggling to find his place in the world. The armed forces and space programs quite rightly have very highly qualified career women working in their departments, and in most aspects of industry, women are excelling. The old male bastions are crumbling and with them their innate self-respect as well as their understanding of how they should act and what they desire.

Any woman reading this may say, "Well, it's a problem for men and they should deal with it." Absolutely, I can reply, but you cannot expect miracles instantly. Generations of history dictating a man's role and function cannot be decided and altered in the space of twenty years without some fallout. Few can argue against the excitement felt by women as their empowerment continues, but at the same time, one must expect issues to coincide with this. And one of those, as I said, is the question of understanding what the modern man is looking for.

Men have started to evolve and are starting to grasp the fact that their role may not be as it once was. "Starting" is the operative word, because this does not mean that there still aren't men who insist on being the breadwinners while their wives remain at home rearing the children. It is going to take a long time to change the world. However, in our Western cities a change is in full swing. Men know that to find a mate they are going to have to work harder than ever before, and they are aware that women call the shots far more than ever before. But this doesn't essentially change what a man is looking for.

Okay, so what is a man seeking?

- First of all, a man is seeking a love interest. This may surprise many women, but men like to love and they like being loved in return. The problem is that many women come across as blasé and cold. It is not easy to find a loving woman, and it is very noticeable how many men try and hang on when they think they have found their Miss Right.
- Men are seeking a woman who is attractive to them. Women may despair that men can be so shallow and that looks could matter so much, but be careful. Men aren't necessarily looking for a catwalk model, and many men don't like women who weigh eighty pounds. But men do want a woman who takes pride in her appearance (though not excessively). Men are proud of having a girlfriend who looks good, and I don't believe any man who says otherwise.
- Men are looking for a trustworthy woman, someone they

can have faith in and who will be there for them. This may sound like an odd thing to say, but the fact is, some women are not trustworthy and many are not faithful either. So many, in fact, that men are increasingly wary. That kiss at a Christmas party or the flirtatious behavior with the gorgeous barman may not count, and in fact it's all great fun and part of a woman's character. But reverse the situation, and as a woman, you hate him doing the same. A man can never forgive a woman being unfaithful, and so he is looking for someone he really does trust.

- Men want to make a home eventually and are looking for a woman who will be willing to share his home life. Women with a sociable lifestyle are attractive because they can be relied upon to keep the social diary running in a long-term relationship.

- Men are seeking women who are feminine, gentle, and kind, because deep down the qualities that make a woman a great mother are an attraction in themselves. I am not suggesting that the man himself needs mothering, though some do; it is more the point that men seek the attributes in women that point to someone who would make a great mother to future offspring.

- Men want women with a great sense of humor. Women often come across as uptight or too bothered by too many small details. You sometimes hear mention of a girl who is "one of the boys." What this means is that she is able to fit in with their humor and is sociable and fun to be with. Such women are extremely attractive to many men. Men want to have a good time and relax when they are not working, so their ideal partners are women who are able to do the same.

- Men are looking for women who retain their femininity and

are caring and kind. A woman can make a fashion statement with the way she dresses. It still doesn't make her more attractive than a kind woman with a good heart and a sweet personality. While every woman in the world burps and farts and has the right to drink pints of beer, it doesn't necessarily attract the opposite sex to her. Women can get angry and say that a man will just have to get used to it, but the issue is that they don't. They can just choose not to go for women who act in the same way as their drinking buddies.

- Men want someone who is supportive. Many women are quick to criticize men in their behavior and career, and set about trying to alter them and mold them. This is a crucial mistake. Men can be manipulated, yes, but they see their partnerships as support systems. The best relationships work both ways in terms of support. Where a woman is not able or willing to give that support and is too quick to criticize, then she may lose her man.

- Men don't like angry women who shout. They want a woman who can debate and converse and discuss. Communication is king. A fiery passionate temperament may have made you interesting and challenging on day one. But by day five hundred it holds no glory whatsoever.

- Men love a challenging woman who keeps them on their toes. Men are generally lazy in relationships once they feel they're in secure territory. When a real man is challenged, he will rise to the occasion. If you want to keep your man interested, keep him challenged.

- One of you will get bored in the bedroom. Men know what they like in bed and tend to stick to it. But when it comes to women, men almost need a thermometer in the bed to check her temperature and her mood to know how to keep her satisfied. A man doesn't like surprises unless he is lying on his back. A word to the wise: Don't try to surprise your man while he is lying on his stomach. I am trying to keep you from getting your neck choked out of you.

- Men want a woman who will commit to them. Though increasingly this is hard to find, it doesn't take away the wish. Men want a girlfriend whom they can share with and trust and be open with. Commitment is not a one-way street and therefore men are struggling to find the levels of commitment they found previously. But the need is still there.

- Men don't want to be alone. If you think I'm lying, why do single men think that they need so many women and why do married men cheat?

About the Author

Born in Oklahoma, "Big Boom" embarked on an unending self-education, which has distinguished him as an authority on harnessing human potential and matters of the heart. Boom's craze to learn and realize greatness helped him achieve a level of honesty about life. He reached out to God and has since gotten on God's path to experiencing life and speaking to women on how to avoid certain pitfalls and experience fulfilling relationships. Boom is the nation's self-proclaimed leading authority on understanding and stimulating human potential in the area of love and relationships. He utilizes powerful delivery and newly emerging insights to teach, inspire, and channel you to new levels of achievement.

Boom works as a personal bodyguard, providing protection for celebrity clients. He also works as the bodyguard for women's hearts, giving talks around the country and selling his relationship advice books aimed at individuals, groups, and organizations. Boom's books provide access into the secrets that men vow never to reveal, because he is dedicated to protecting women and their hearts. Boom thrives on speaking to women's groups all over the country.

Boom lives in Texas with his family.

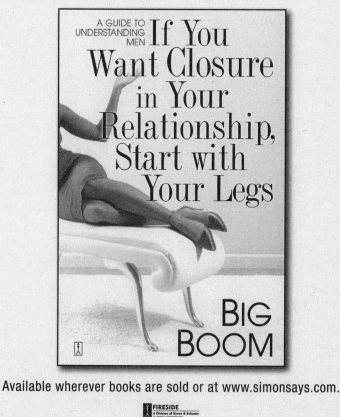